The Rise of Multipartyism
and Democracy in the
Context of Global Change

The Rise of Multipartyism and Democracy in the Context of Global Change

The Case of Africa

Tukumbi Lumumba-Kasongo

Westport, Connecticut
London

Library of Congress Cataloging-in-Publication Data

Lumumba-Kasongo, Tukumbi, 1948–
    The rise of multipartyism and democracy in the context of global
change : the case of Africa / Tukumbi Lumumba-Kasongo.
      p. cm.
    Includes bibliographical references and index.
    ISBN 0–275–96087–0 (alk. paper)
    1. Political parties—Africa. 2. Democracy—Africa. 3. Africa—
Politics and government—1960– I. Title.
JQ1879.A795L86   1998
320.96′09′045—DC21   97–34753

British Library Cataloguing in Publication Data is available.

Library of Congress Catalog Card Number: 97–34753
ISBN: 0–275–96087–0

First published in 1998

Praeger Publishers, 88 Post Road West, Westport, CT 06881
An imprint of Greenwood Publishing Group, Inc.

Printed in the United States of America

The paper used in this book complies with the
Permanent Paper Standard issued by the National
Information Standards Organization (Z39.48–1984).

10 9 8 7 6 5 4 3 2 1

Contents

In memory of my uncle Papa Dr. Pierre Shaumba and his beloved wife Maman Thérèse Shaumba, who inspired me.

Preface

It is my view that the current applications of the concepts of liberal democracy, multipartyism, and development in Africa must be re-defined because they have created faulty perceptions of social change, unrealizable expectations, and irrelevant political practices. They have de facto been perceived as synonymous. In reality, they are not and should not be. These concepts need to be demystified, both epistemologically and politically, so that they can better serve Africa in concrete political situations in the 21st century and beyond within the global system.

I had been thinking about writing a book on multipartyism and democracy since 1982 while I was teaching and chairing the department of political science at University of Liberia in Monrovia, Liberia. The specific events that triggered the work on this book project were the treatment of opposition parties and the manipulation of the rules of the game between 1984 and 1985 by the late Samuel K. Doe, the head of state of Liberia, when he decided to run for the presidency. As expected in an African context, few rules were followed. The idea was enriched while I spent several months in Dakar, Senegal, mostly at *The Institut du Développement Economique et de Plannification* (IDEP, A United Nations Specialized Training Agency) and also in Abidjan, Côte d'Ivoire in early 1992. Here, I observed the process of the new political era with the intensification of popular actions from the opposition parties in Abidjan, especially at *Université Nationale de* Côte d'Ivoire (now *Université de* Cocody). During this period, in Abidjan, I conducted research that led to a paper entitled: "What do the Opposition Parties want?" I was also involved in another research project in the explosive situation of the rise of political parties in the former Zaïre (now the Democratic Republic of Congo).

While in Abidjan, where I have been an Associate Researcher at the *Institut d'Ethnosociologie* at the *Université Nationale de* Côte d'Ivoire, I had the chance to discuss often the nature of the opposition parties in Côte d'Ivoire with colleagues and students on campus. When I came back to Cornell University on May 1, 1992, I presented my research results in a well-attended seminar of the Institute for African

Development (IAD) on the Ivorian and several other African countries.

Several parts of this book were presented in conferences and seminars in Africa, the U.S.A., and Europe, including an extensive interview on the Radio Dutch Welle while I was attending the International Political Science Congress in Berlin (Germany) in 1994. I benefited a lot from comments from colleagues who participated in the African Association of Political Science Biennial Congress in Ibadan, Nigeria in August 1995 where a chapter on "The Role of the Church in democratic process" was presented. The chapter on "Ethnicity" was read in Harare, Zimbabwe, in a conference organized by the International Political Science Association, Section on Political Philosophy also in August 1995.

It should be noted that the first draft of the manuscript of this book was accepted before the end of Mobutu's tyranny in the Democratic Republic of Congo. However, given the level of political oppression and economic malaise in the country and Mobutu's resistance to make genuine political reforms, my analysis predicted that popular movements against Mobutu were moving toward a higher critical stage, that is, mobilization of political violence unprecedented in the history of popular struggle in the DRC. My arguments are still valid even when Mobutu died in Morocco as a villain.

I thank the participants in these meetings for their constructive comments. I thank also *Professeur* Lanciné Sylla of Université de Cocody, then the director of the *Institut d'Ethnosocologie*, and *Professeur* Kwamé N'Guessan, a friend and colleague at the same Institute, for their comments and profound knowledge of the local political environment that benefited me. I thank also Mr. Ben M'poko, a compatriot from the Democratic Republic of Congo, for his contribution to my research in Abidjan. I thank also *Professeur* Francis Wodié of Université de Cocody (Faculty of Law) and the General Secretary of the *Parti Ivoirien du Travail* (PIT) for an interview that Mô N'Dri and I had with him in Abidjan in July 1993. My deep and most sincere gratitude goes to all the Lumumba-Kasongos (members of my family) for their patience and love that allowed me to produce this book on an important subject of this decade on time.

I would also like to extend my sincere thanks to Ms. Janet Mapstone who, despite her very busy schedule as a graphic designer at Wells College and the tight scrutiny of my production editors, has finalized the typesetting of the manuscript. In setting it up in Pagemaker, all the necessary corrections requested or suggested by the production editors were made through her office.

Finally, it is needless to emphasize that all the contradictions and mal-interpretation are those of the author alone.

Abbreviations

ADF	*Alliance pour la Démocratie et la Fédération*
ADFLC	The Alliance of the Democratic Forces for Liberation of Congo
ANC	African National Congress
CAR	Central African Republic
CCM	Chama Cha Mapinduzi
CODESA	Convention of Democratic South Africa
FCN	*Front Commun des Nationalistes*
FIS	*Front Islamique du Salut*
FORUM	Forum for the Restoration of Democracy
FPI	*Front Populaire Ivorien*
GDP	Gross Domestic Product
GNP	Gross National Product
IMF	International Monetary Fund
KANU	Kenya African National Union
LCC	Liberian Council of Churches
LPA	Lagos Plan of Action
MDP	*Mouvement des Démocrates et Patriotes*
MDS	*Mouvement Démocratique et Social*
MNC/L	*Mouvement National Congolais/Lumumba*
MOJA	Movement for Justice in Africa
MPR	*Mouvement Populaire de la Révolution*
NCCK	National Council of Churches of Kenya
NDA	National Democratic Alliance in the Sudan
NP	National Party
NRC	National Republican Convention
PASP	Pan-African Socialist Party
PDCI	*Parti Démocratique de Côte d'Ivoire*
PDSC	*Parti Démocratique et Social Chrétien*
PFA	*Parti de la Fédération Africaine*

PIT	*Parti Ivorien du Travail*
PSI	*Parti Socialiste Ivoirien*
RDA	*Rassemblement Démocratique Africain*
RDR	*Rassemblement Démocratique de République*
SAPs	Structural Adjustment Programs
SDP	Sudan Democratic Party
SWAPO	South West African People's Organization
UDP	United Democratic Party
UDPS	*Union pour la Démocratie et le Progrès Social*
UNDD	*Union Nationale pour la Défense de Démocratie*
US	*Union Sacrée*
U.S.	United States
USD	*Union Sociale Démocratique*

The Rise of Multipartyism and Democracy in the Context of Global Change

1

Introduction: Issues, Approaches, and Theoretical Considerations

In Africa, since the early 1990s, multipartyism has become one of the most commonly debated issues and valuable characteristics of political reforms, popular movements, and power struggles. Multiparty elections have become popular and routine: over 40 have successfully or unsuccessfully taken place. Furthermore, in 1996 and 1997, many new African democracies, such as Bénin, Burkina Faso, Côte d'Ivoire, Guinea-Conakry, Mali, and Togo, conducted their second elections. Indeed, 1991 was the starting point in a new wave of multiparty democracy in Africa; to some degree, this movement has hope—creating momentum similar to that of the 1960s.

However, despite the visibility of political pluralism in the African news media and in informal discussions and forums, until recently scholars and international institutions did not focus on its impact and implications as they did in studying the Structural Adjustment Programs of the World Bank and the International Monetary Fund (IMF). Yet the dynamics of multipartyism has shaped local African politics in a way that is clearly unprecedented since the 1960s.

The study of multipartyism and democracy, as they are defined in Africa and organized by African social forces and states, will help us understand not only the nature of African politics but also the dynamics of global change at the subsystem level of the world system. Thus, this study will enrich our understanding of democratic practices and values.

This book has five major interrelated objectives:

1. to examine and understand the dynamics of recent multiparty politics, their social, political, and policy implications, and their impact on various social forces in Africa— political opposition parties, ethnicity and nationalism, and the church, for example.
2. to discuss how opposition parties have conceived and defined democracy.
3. to analyze militarism as an important associative political phenomenon that should not be counted out in African politics.
4. to see whether or not multipartyism can survive in the post–Cold War Era in Africa.
5. to determine whether there are any significant or positive correlations between

multipartyism, the practical significance of existing democracies, and the struggle for social progress and justice.

The achievements of these objectives will answer three major questions: What is the social relevance of the democratization process? What kind of society have popular movements and political parties been articulating? Are legislative and presidential elections enough to create conditions for social progress to occur among the majority of people?

In short, this book theorizes about democracy within a broad perspective; it attempts to identify its general characteristics as they are actually experienced and expressed in an African context by various social groups and communities. In other words, it offers an interpretation of democracy as it is manifested in Africa. Multipartyism is popularly perceived among various social groups, especially the elites, as the most legitimate way to transfer, share, or to capture power. It has become *à la mode* ("fashionable") to talk about multipartyism as another form of nationalism or as an expression of democracy. This instrument of social change has been considered by various elites in political parties, and by the ordinary people, as a means to challenge the state or ruling parties: it is perceived as a "war" against African dictatorships and the rich people. In general terms, people are being mobilized to support multipartyism both regionally and locally.

Between the end of the 1950s and 1996, the dynamics of both African social and political conditions and world politics produced many successful military coup d'états in Africa. Contemporary African societies and their politics have been shaped more by the history of dictatorship and its political culture than by any efforts towards direct systematic democratization. Although there have been some islands of civilian regimes that had some liberal democratic institutions and were not militarily structured, until recently, post-colonial Africa could be characterized as essentially non-democratic and without a functioning multiparty system.

Multiparty politics, however, are not a totally new concept in Africa. Various forms of multiparty politics, as reflected in nationalistic political expressions, such as "uhuru" (independence), "Africa for Africans," the search for "African personality," and "self-determination" flourished before and immediately after the independence of many countries. However, for various reasons, as is examined later in this book, multipartyism did not last for long before it was crushed. Suddenly, it has again become part of the popular lexicon. As Michael Bratton stated:

What is new and exciting—to African citizens and political analysts alike—is the return of politics to daily life. For the first time in a generation, Africans now generally feel free to speak their minds publicly and to form political associations outside the confines of official control. And, in many countries, African voters have enjoyed the opportunity to exercise the long denied right to choose leaders in genuinely competitive polls.[1]

This view is only partially correct, and the meaning of this statement has to be examined within the context of global politics. What do genuinely competitive elections mean for the ordinary poor people, for instance, in Algeria, Côte d'Ivoire,

Nigeria, Tanzania, Senegal, or Zimbabwe?

Although in the 1990s, in many African countries, such as Cameroon, Gabon, Guinea-Conakry, Kenya, the Sudan, Togo, and Zaïre (now the Democratic Republic of Congo), the heads of state have clung to power, they have substantially lost the aura of divine power they enjoyed in the past.

Another phenomenon that many people, including experts on African development, tend to associate with the rise of multipartyism in Africa is the quest for a new basis for development and social progress. There are those who strongly believe that Africa has produced and/or inherited development models that did not work or have not yet fully matured. This point of view may not be convincing; however, after the failures of the nationalistic and militaristic based policies of the new African petty bourgeoisie of the 1960s and 1970s, the majority of the African population, especially farmers, peasants, the working classes, women, and the lumpen-proletarians, are looking for new ways of survival in an extremely difficult international and national socioeconomic and political environment. For many people, despite skepticism based on their past political and social experiences, multipartyism and democracy are strongly associated with the improvement of individual and collective social and economic conditions.

In 1980, some African dictators and a few enlightened heads of state like Julius Nyerere of Tanzania produced the Lagos Plan of Action (LPA) to search for a new policy basis for the development of the continent. However, the plan, which called for self-determination and self-sufficiency in food production, was never implemented because of the nature of the African leadership and the structure of its economic and political relationships with the countries in the North.

Despite analytical and historical concerns raised by scholars about the philosophical and political assumptions of linking development to democracy and the lack of empirical data to consistently support such assumptions in specific cases in Africa, most students of politics and political economy agree that there cannot be any broad development or social transformation in any society until its people fully participate in the process of its construction. As the late Claude Ake maintains:

Democracy requires even development, otherwise it cannot give equal opportunities to all, it cannot incorporate all to articulate their interests to negotiate them. It cannot produce a political community in which all are able to enjoy rights, nor avoid compromising justice because it takes the development of consciousness and capabilities to seek and enjoy justice. That is why development especially even development in this broad sense, is an integral part of the process of democratization. (1992, 50)

Recently, many people in Africa have come to believe that the time has arrived for such participation. For many, the national and international environment is conducive to the dialogue between democracy and development. The demands for popular participation, and the long history of the people's struggles against dictatorships, are taken as important steps toward realizing democracy. As Jacques Mariel Nzounakeu stated:

The demands for multiparty systems that are being made today are therefore an attempt by the African countries to claim democracy through other means. . . . But aside from this argument, most African countries see the multiparty system as a way of stimulating ideological debate, improving human rights, increasing democracy and finally, as a means of accelerating economic and social development.[2]

Popular movements and multiparty politics, both of which demand an open political process, participation, power sharing, fair distribution of resources, and the protection of people's social and political rights, are seriously challenging the power of the African state, its policies, and its legitimacy. Although this challenge may not necessarily be ideological, it is forcing the state to make some concessions. Indeed, African states cannot continue to be indifferent to internal demands and international pressures. The dynamics of political reforms in Namibia and South Africa, for instance, has been the result of both internal and external power configurations.

Recently the relationships between the state, society, and the economy have been manifested in the form of antinomy.[3] This situation has become clearer than ever, particularly between the state and society in the post-colonial era, due to the fact that the majority of African people have become poorer in absolute and relative terms due to many factors, among which the most important are state inefficiency, corruption, malpractice in the process of surplus accumulation, structural inequality in the mechanisms of distribution, and administrative dysfunctionality. Furthermore, the role that Africa had been assigned by the forces of the world system: colonial powers, capitalists, and their local allies to play in the international market for the past hundred years is becoming more inefficient than ever; and it is anachronistic for both the North and the South. Despite a recent (1994–1997) modest overall improvement in economic growth in Africa, in 1995, it was estimated that there were about 300 million poor people out of the estimated 625 million in Africa. About 210 million (as of 1997) of these were extremely poor. There are other statistics that show that over half of the population of subSaharan Africa lives in "absolute poverty" on less than $1 day (Novicki, 1997, 5). These figures do not include recently displaced people or refugees. It is estimated that Africa, as of 1994, had 7 million refugees, a third of the world's total, and some 21 million people who were internally displaced.[4] Unfortunately, this number is not consistently decreasing.

Poverty, a very complex phenomenon, is defined by the lack of resources, of a productive and creative life, and of the necessary means to live a decent, healthy life. It is not narrowly or technically measured by per capita income, caloric intake, or savings. It is not a natural product of the evolution of a given people or society. The majority of African people, especially the poorest of the poor, have been alienated by the state and have responded with anger, hostility, and struggle. Moreover, they have developed ambiguous views concerning the mission of the state. In some countries, such as Sudan, Sierra Leone, or the Democratic Republic of Congo, observers describe the masses of people (in their relationship to the state) as being in a Hobbesian state of nature or "resigned" to being poor. In reality, people do not resign themselves to being poor. However, material resources have become less available, and the state, with its patron-client regime, has become more authoritarian and selective in managing its scarce resources and its citizens—ironically, even within the framework of existing democratic and popular movements. In addition, in many countries for a long time in post-colonial Africa, political instability did not allow individual initiative to develop, grow, and mature. An angry person knows no laws, order, or politics. What matters for a sick person is medicine. Animosity toward the state is a function of the relationship between people's expectations of what the state should do (duty and obligation) and its actual performance, which is often irrational and irresponsible. The state's reactions to demands for political reforms such as multipartyism or societal changes vary from strong or partial resistance to accommodation or reluctant acceptance.

In the African context, popular movements are defined as coalitions of various movements and organizations, which articulate social and political issues, generally in non-ideological terms. They have the potential power to advance history, although not necessarily toward a realization of a concrete national agenda or social revolutionary objectives. In the past 30 to 40 years, Africa has consistently been the scene of popular demonstrations, strikes, and protests. In the past, these uprisings have led to the collapse or change of regime in some countries (for instance, Ghana, Mali, and the Sudan). By the early 1990s, for instance, Daniel arap Moi, the president of Kenya and his government were seriously challenged by political opposition and popular movements. To understand the dynamic conditions that might lead to a regime's collapse, a combination of factors within the local context and international environment must be taken into account.

In their behavior, popular movements are often spontaneous without necessarily having strong, clear ideological or philosophical bases. Still, they are capable of creating the momentum for a long-term struggle for societal change. In Africa, they are generally organized by strong, charismatic leaders, who tend to become idolized and undemocratic. The effectiveness of their actions and policies depends a great deal on their ability to mobilize people and on the socio-cultural context in which the movement operates. In short, they are contributing to the current process of political redefinition in Africa by creating space in which the state and society can enter into a dialogue. Have they been able to enter into this dialogue?

Many scholars in the West are dealing with popular movements in Africa in a symptomatic way. To some, the dramatic changes that started to occur in African politics appeared quite suddenly. The assumption behind this kind of reasoning has been that the conditions in Africa and its societies, by themselves, cannot produce genuine political movements that can lead to meaningful changes. This reasoning implies that what recently has been happening in Africa does not necessarily have its origin in African social structures and political economies. By 1997, most African states had adopted multipartyism as a form of power sharing. More than two-thirds of the African states (or about 48 states) have either already revised their constitutions to accommodate the multiparty movement or have seriously engaged in public debates on the issue. Many have established new electoral codes. From the West, as Issa Shivji noted, the domino theory provides an explanation for this change: "Thirty years later, we are told, there is a wind of change. The origin of the wind, we are told, lies in Eastern Europe. The mentors of change, as always, are from the West, including the erstwhile IMF/World Bank."[5]

The perception of the theory above is ahistorical. Thus, it tends to denigrate the efforts of the popular struggles that have stood against autocratic totalitarian rulers in Africa over the past 40 years. For instance, student protests, working-class strikes, market women's demonstrations, and progressive intellectuals' public discourses, have almost continuously threatened the ruling classes' interests at different times in countries such as Algeria, Bénin, Cameroon, the Central African Republic (CAR), Chad, Côte d'Ivoire, Gabon, Ghana, Liberia, Mali, Morocco, Nigeria, Togo, South Africa, the Sudan, and the Democratic Republic of Congo. In fact, one could say that the people's confrontation with those states is ongoing. Although in most cases they did not bring down the government, partially because they did not have the material means or organizations to do so, they have contributed to the demystification of the regimes and the diminution of their power and public image.

On the other hand, in formal terms, multipartyism, as an expression of political pluralism within a liberal democracy, is a political situation in which a given constitutional arrangement, or the political elite, allow several functioning political parties to compete for legislative and presidential offices. It is a situation in which civil society becomes a potential instrument for influencing policy formation and, consequently, of social progress. In theory, it offers several options on how to govern or be governed. In Africa, some people are members of popular movements and multiparty formation at the same time—they represent both social forces. This does not mean that there is necessarily a political identity crisis. Rather, this flexibility is a reflection of the nature of African social relations and society. Indeed, in the same family, there may be Muslims, Christians, and those who believe in African religions. They usually co-exist without too much tension. That is, whereas multiparty politics emerged differently in Africa than in Europe, it tends to contain a universal message. Multipartyism is defined as the freedom of individual citizens to create as many political parties as they wish according to the law. Consequently, in some countries there are a great number of political parties: in 1995, for instance, in Bénin, there were as many as 150 political parties.

The recent struggle for democracy is rooted in contextual conditions, and the democratic movements should be examined both contextually and historically. The fall of the Berlin Wall in November 1989 and the Eastern European movements only helped to accelerate and internationalize a process that has local origins. Discussion of the dynamism of political pluralism or the struggle for democracy must take into account the specificities of local conditions and culture, as well as the forces that have fostered such a struggle.

Political pluralism, as defined by modernization theorists, who perceive the behavior of various members of the elite, especially the upper middle classes (technocrats, bureaucrats, and business groups), and their notion of consensus as an expression of democracy cannot help us fully appreciate the significance of the struggle for democracy, as this struggle is articulated by various progressive and popular forces in Africa. Competition among the elite for public offices and in the market place, and their input in the functioning of the parliament, may not tell us much about the meaning of democracy.

The key issues in political pluralism in Africa should be the mechanisms of the distribution of power and resource management, and their policy implications. The question of equity is an important ethical consideration for an analysis of democratic discourses. The majority of Africans tend to perceive democracy in ethical and developmental terms. Given the poverty in most parts of the continent among certain social classes and ethnic groups, the issue of the distribution of resources is vital to the current functioning of pluralistic democracy. Multipartyism is not in itself a strong instrument that is philosophically capable of provoking structural changes (social transformation) if the democracy in question does not involve accountability, respect for the right to life, the quest for social equality, and collective responsibility. That is to say, conceptually, for people, democracy may be more valuable than multipartyism. Thus, political pluralism should not simply be defined as a descriptive or technical expression of various elite groups or a normative behavior of the political elite and their prescribed attitudes in a given society. Rather, it has to be seen as a normative and prescriptive phenomenon.

One of the important goals of this book is to analyze the objectives of the institutionalization of opposition parties. In relationship to political opposition, political pluralism in Africa is an expression of the power struggle. It is an arena where the opposition wants to be heard and wants to capture state power. It is in this political space also that policy disagreements are debated. However, the real struggle for democracy that has a long-term constructive objective, whether it originates from genuine legal opposition or popular movements, is the one that articulates people's needs and interests for the promotion of human equality and progress. In this regard, Ilunga Kabongo, as cited by F. Scott Bobb, adds other elements to the definition of democracy: "Democracy is not to be equated with just the ritual of voting and elections, but is rather the coexistence of a plurality of opinions guaranteed by freedom of expression under the rule of the majority, the rulers being basically accountable for their actions to this majority" (1988, 170).

An important issue is how political pluralism and democratization produce actions for positive change. Between the second half of the 1940s and the early 1960s, African conditions, and their internal contradictions in each sub-region or country, produced various forms of political organizations and movements. Regardless of the specific conditions that led to the creation of specific organizations, and the political history of different African states, multipartyism at the national level quickly collapsed in the 1960s as new states tried to become a part of world capitalism without consciously adopting a liberal democratic form of government. Through the ritual of elections and the international demand for national stability, the African elite quickly opted for a monopoly of power, hoping to acquire more resources from both national and international sectors to support their governments. Many regimes became incapable of converting inputs (demands) into policies due to many institutional, ideological, and political constraints. The process of monopolizing power has been sine qua non for the survival of capitalism in non-liberal democratic states. The various processes of integration helped the states become authoritarian, totalitarian, and autocratic in the name of the nation-building process. Why have the overwhelming majority of neo-colonial states in Africa been incapable of producing relevant political pluralism and democracy through which people can effectively participate in their social and political affairs?

The colonial states in Africa were essentially militaristic, anti-democratic, absolutely arbitrary, and absolutely powerful (Lumumba-Kasongo, 1991a). Their policies were formulated and implemented from the perspective of domination. However, even if some limited political participation was gradually introduced and later promoted, either in the so-called indirect British rule or in the French type of direct rule, the process did not become routine within the local political structures and practices of the colonial administrations. This limited participation did not transform either the political philosophy of colonialism or the nature of the decision making institutions. Wherever such a limited participation was possible, it was used as an instrument of states to advance and support the colonial political economy and its values.

Colonial politics did not change on their own. The intensity of the various forms of popular movements, including the progressive social and political forces in the metropolitan countries, the consequences of the imperialist wars (World Wars I and II), and the colonial powers' needs for modernizing colonialism (the main objective being to make it economically more efficient and enduring) led colonial powers to reformulate some of their policies with the intention of continuing to rule. The political and social reforms introduced were reflected in local political institutions: for example, in elections of Africans to the local administrative and district offices and in the beginning of debate on the question of autonomy in some countries. For instance, in deciding to first grant autonomy the French colonies in Africa, and later grant independence, Charles de Gaulle, for instance, wished to protect the "immortality" of France in Africa. His deliberate approach was to avoid, as much as possible, the consolidation of national power struggles that could lead to revolution.

This kind of political participation, as practiced either in the French National Assembly or in local governments, was based on the assumption of an ambiguous and artificial form of liberal democracy. Upon independence, most, if not all, new African states adopted parliamentary democracy. This representative democracy was popular but was not clearly understood in terms of the history of its formation and the nature of its requirements. While it took the Burkinabè, Ghanaian, Ivorian, Nigerian, and Senegalese elite, for instance, five to ten years to learn and practice their adopted or imposed parliamentary systems, it took less than one year for the Congolese (Zaïrean) elite to learn and practice the values of their adopted democracy. Although the time frame for full implementation of liberal democracy does not necessarily determine the quality of democracy, it can illustrate how a democracy has penetrated the existing institutions and value system at a given moment.

Can multipartyism, as currently defined and practiced in Africa, produce both democracy and social progress? Does it contain some elements of democracy?

Can it nurture the growth of democracy, including the development of democratic institutions and values? What is the difference, for example, between multiparty politics in Bénin, Burkina Faso, Cameroon, the Congo, Kenya, Malawi, Nigeria, and Togo today and the one-party state in the same countries in the past?

In 1990, after the release of President Nelson Mandela from the prison where he spent 27 years, Mathieu Kérékou's defeat in 1991 (in May 1996, he was re-elected president of the Republic of Bénin), and his departure from the political scene following the Bénin national conference, the uprisings in Côte d'Ivoire and Togo, and the implementation of multipartyism there, popular movements have manifested themselves in almost every corner in Africa. Although their origins, the quality of the contents of their actions, ideologies, and social specificities of the milieux in which they are operating cannot be generalized, their claims, in many ways, have a similar tone.

The year 1991 can be proclaimed the starting point in the new wave of multiparty democracy in Africa. To a certain extent, it has a momentum similar to that of the 1960s. The surprise result of the November 1, 1991 presidential election in Zambia in which Mr. Frederick Chiluba, the most prominent leader of labor unions and the Movement for Multiparty Democracy (MMD), won with about 85 percent of the popular vote (despite the fact that we still have not been able to understand in an exact and critical way the nature of the international forces' involvement behind the whole process) confirms the point that, if left alone, African people are capable of choosing their own leaders based on their own criteria. Moreover, African political leaders are not religiously supported by the African people. Chiluba was elected primarily by coalitions of labor unions and active rural organizations. Similarly, in the Republic of Bénin in early 1991, Mathieu Kérékou was defeated by his own prime minister, Nicéphore Soglo, although in April 1996, Kérékou unexpectedly reclaimed the presidency. And Sassou Nguesso of the Congo (Congo-Brazzaville) was also defeated in the July 1992 presidential race in which Pascal Lissouba of the Pan-African Socialist Party (PASP) won. In Mali, Moussa Traoré was ousted by an angry and hungry mob before he was judged by the court. Konaré was elected with the support of the masses. In spite of protests from the opposition parties, he was also re-elected president in May 1997. Moreover, in the CAR, Ange Pattassé, bras droit ("right hand man") of the former self-made emperor, Jean-Bendel Bokassa, defeated President André Kolingba in the presidential elections of September and October 1993. Moussa Traoré was found guilty of depleting public funds and sentenced to death in February 1993. In April 1994, Nelson Mandela of the African National Congress (ANC) defeated Frederick N. de Klerk of the National Party (NP), the last old ruling party, in a presidential race that could not have been predicted five years previously. Thus, Mandela became the first president of a democratic South Africa elected through a multiparty democracy that was partially negotiated between political forces and organizations.

Finally, the defeat of Hastings Kamuzu Banda by Bakili Muluzi of the United Democratic Party (UDP) in Malawi's first multiparty presidential elections in May of 1994 is a statement about the readiness and willingness of the African people to change their regimes. Banda ruled Malawi for more than three decades after the country gained its independence from Britain in 1964.

African conditions have produced highly personalized executive presidencies, which have deeply affected the way states have functioned. People perceive states to be the same as presidents or heads of state. Indeed, an excessive personification characterized African politics even where there were strong national revolutionary backgrounds, as in Guinea-Conakry, Guinea-Bissau, and Mozambique, until the emergence of recent popular movements many of which have little unified ideological basis. Without necessarily any clear success, this personification is being seriously challenged. As already indicated, as of 1995, debates about democracy have become almost a routine, spontaneous, natural phenomenon, and presidential and legislative elections have been organized in most parts of the continent.

However, the major question in this analysis is whether the neo-colonial state, its structures (the state bureaucracies and state agencies), and its political economy can create conditions that are conducive to the establishment of genuine (social) democracy. In other words, what is the relationship between political independence, democracy, and society? What is the significance of freedom and human rights without economic self-sufficiency and self-reliance? What is the correlation between democracy and society (culture and values)? What does the fact that people are electing their own leaders mean to these people? Does this have any potential of having a direct, positive impact on their economic and social lives or on their decisions to engage in activities they consider to be profitable, valuable, or important? Can authoritarian or totalitarian politics and poor economic conditions be conducive to real democratic debates?

A general observation is that, historically and philosophically, no country, people, or nation has succeeded in acquiring democracy in meaningful social and economic ways without first becoming ontologically politically independent. Moreover, independence, as perceived either from the state's or the people's perspective, cannot be earned without some form of cultural, political, or economic struggle. Are African countries, states, and people sufficiently independent or prepared to consistently carry on their struggle for democracy? Within existing social and economic conditions, can people, through their current movements, really struggle to promote a true social democracy? Can a poor people have sufficient strength and firm enough principles to struggle for its freedom? The analysis of the correlation between independence and democracy depends, first, on how one defines these terms and, second, on the historical configurations in which they are supposed to operate.

The struggle for democracy has taken different forms across Africa. The nature of its manifestations and the energies behind it depend on the nature and level of local social contradictions and how those contradictions relate to the international and global political economy, as well as on how democracy is perceived within such a social milieu. Recently, the African intelligentsia has incorporated this theme in its research and scholarly activities,[6] rural women have continued to organize cooperatives in many countries, students and bureaucrats have organized themselves through formal political or social organizations, and the working classes have consolidated their demands through labor unions. The permanent lumpen-proletarians, unpaid workers, and women and men from the "informal sector" in many urban areas have taken to the streets to protest state policies. The spontaneous coalitions that have taken place among all of these social classes, though fragile by nature, have produced popular movements. Most African states reacted violently against these movements, as in Cameroon, Equatorial Guinea, Nigeria, Togo, and the Democratic Republic of Congo, but in the end, in many cases, a compromise or a new governance formula has been reached, whether or not all classes agreed with its content. This has been the case in Bénin, Côte d'Ivoire, Cameroon, Congo-Brazzaville, Ghana, Kenya, Mali, Niger, and Zambia.

The struggle for democracy in Africa cannot be defined or reduced simply to the struggle of having access to political power or control of the state's resources, as traditionally perceived by students of politics, but, more importantly, it is the right to live well in one's social milieu (social rights). In many cases, this struggle can also be considered the struggle to disengage from neo-colonial state programs and agendas.

The view elaborated here is that a real democratic right is by essence a developmental right. In the absence of any functioning democracy, Claude Ake wonders whether development has even started in Africa. As previously mentioned, in this case, development is not narrowly defined as an increase in per capita income. In a broader concept of development, one that incorporates the general well-being of the population at large and basic civil and political freedoms, a democracy that insures these freedoms, by definition, can be more conducive to development than can a non-democratic regime. It is the struggle against oppressive conditions and forces imposed on society by the state (1996, 18–41). Objectives that are claimed by many of those who are involved in these democratic movements are not technically determined by the processes that state has created for promoting its own interests. Rather, they are broad and, consequently, must be analyzed.

Many movements have their origin in the structure of African states as well as in the structure and functioning of peripheral capitalism. The excessive use of power by a small elite to articulate its own interests, and the poverty of the majority of the people, have created uncommunicated and uneasy relations between the state, the peripheral capitalist political economy, and the people. External factors, which include the process of the internationalization of labor, the accumulation of surpluses, the control of resources by multinationals, and the power struggle between the North and South, also must be taken into account. The crisis of peripheral capitalism, reflected by its failure to deliver, is another real determinant factor that has led to the rise of popular movements. Most of these movements demand the equal distribution of national resources, more participation in the affairs of society, protection of basic human and social rights, land distribution, and power sharing.

Democratic movements have exploded in the period in which, despite substantial resistance, the majority of the African states have adopted the SAPs of the World Bank and the stabilization programs of the IMF and their conditionalities into their domestic public policies. The African debt, which was $200 billion in 1993, reached over $210 billion in 1995; debt service in many countries takes more than 30 percent of their exports. Furthermore, the decline of commodity prices has continued to frustrate individual and state planning and the purchasing power of many people, especially those in rural areas, thus producing social disasters. As of 1994, despite combined efforts by donors to improve the quality of their relations with African states and business communities and the prospects of socio-economic transformation generated by the SAPs of the World Bank and the IMF, the general conditions of the majority of people are not very promising.

In addition, in the past, the militarization of politics since the mid-1960s, as reflected in the rigidity, totalitarianism, and authoritarianism of the African state, alienated most people from effectively participating in the public sector in order to save it from a total collapse. The public sector has been, as it is called in Liberia, "our elephant"—a collective place to steal faster. Not surprisingly, people tend to have less confidence in this system than in their own businesses. In light of a high level of corruption in the governance systems in many countries, the public sector has become even more unreliable. In short, one can make some general correlations between African political and socio-economic crises and the rise of popular movements.

As indicated earlier, nearly four decades after the majority of African countries gained their political independence, the social and economic conditions of the majority of the population are not getting any better. On the contrary, in most cases, they are getting worse. Students of the African political economy and international and multilateral organizations agree that the living conditions of ordinary people, and even those of the so-called middle classes, have deteriorated more than 40 percent since the 1960s. Poverty rates have also increased within all social classes. Through popular and democratic movements, people's efforts have been focused on the question of the abilities or inabilities and the legitimacy or illegitimacy of the African ruling classes and states to continue to rule, as well as on how to improve people's conditions. Their efforts are part of the search for the real meaning of African independence.

From the above discussion, one can distinguish between two social phenomena that are simultaneously taking place in many countries: the struggle for democracy, political participation, and the right to live well; and the struggle against neo-colonialism (called also the new independence movement). There is a consensus among African political economists that neo-colonial states have produced a virtual re-colonization of Africa by the industrial powers and international and multilateral financial institutions. During the Cold War, policies used by the African states and foreign powers to maintain underdevelopment, as reflected in people's conditions, were the symptoms of this virtual re-colonization of Africa. Many popular movements, which are coalitions of various social forces, are raising those issues through violent struggle. As a result, a second or third independence movement is taking place in many parts of Africa.

The above issues do not diminish the importance or visibility of the rise of multiparty politics and popular movements. The actions of popular movements and political parties are forcing scholars, students of Africa, and even some donors in the industrialized countries to take the study of democracy seriously and to carefully analyze the claims of its advocates. Even the World Bank and the IMF have added democracy to their conditionalities for access to loans and grants.

Among the questions that must be addressed are the following: Is it possible for these ongoing popular movements to produce some form of participatory political system? Are participatory systems a necessary prerequisite for social progress in Africa? Can political democracy effectively preserve and enhance African cultures for development or social progress and industrialization objectives without democratizing the whole society?

In the context of this book, understanding the nature of political arrangements and their characteristics, and democratic theories in Africa, promotes understanding of African conditions, political cultures, and the need for development. The kinds of democratic theories that can provoke positive changes at the local or national level and influence contemporary regional and international relations and politics is another component of the debate that is indirectly addressed in this book. Answering that question requires analysis of those theories and their sociological and political impacts. The exercise is basically theoretical, although concrete examples based on historical and policy-oriented perspectives illustrate and clarify points.

No scholarship can simultaneously provide a full understanding of all the above questions. However, these questions raise important issues and provide an intellectual and political perspective needed for further comprehension of the dynamics of new political forces in Africa. What can, will, or should the current popular movements and multipartyism in Africa practically achieve within the context of the new international political and economic environment in which they are operating? Has the external factor (global capitalism and foreign policy in the North) left Africa alone to take care of its malaise with its own means? Could African political leaders like Mathieu Kérékou of Bénin, Kenneth Kaunda of Zambia, Sassou Nguesso of the Congo, Kamuzu Banda of Malawi, and de Klerk of South Africa, for instance, be defeated through a democratic process without the so-called blessing of international and foreign financial institutions? Can democracy be taken seriously at the local and national level without having economic correspondence at the international level?

This is not the first time movements that claim to struggle for democracy and independence have emerged in Africa. In the past, movements such as Kitawala, Maji-Maji, Mulelism, and many other forms of national liberation movements, each with its own local particularities, have struggled for political independence or for the advancement of some form of just society in their respective countries. Although their spirit has probably survived today because the conditions that engendered them have not qualitatively changed much, most of them were militarily crushed by the colonial and neo-colonial powers. However, the "warrior tradition," to borrow Ali Mazrui's expression, is still alive and well in many African cultures, but will it produce a relevant functional democracy?

Political leaders such as Félix Houphouët-Boigny, Jomo Kenyatta, Patrice Lumumba, Kwame Nkrumah, Julius Nyerere, Samora Machel, and Léopold Sédar Senghor also articulated the idea of national political independence as a *sine qua non* for African progress. Although nationalism does not necessarily lead to the establishment of democracy, it implies that people, with their nationalistic spirit, may be willing to bring their input to the processes of state- or nation-building and governance. History, however, testifies that the so-called state democracy is not the same as genuine representative or people's democracy for society at large.

In the past, state democracy was generally a practice created by the actions of the elite to gain, manage, and retain power. It can thus be characterized as a self-delegating system. The state appoints itself as the spokesperson for the whole society. Although it might promote reconciliation with society on some specific policy issues in order to establish its own basis of legitimacy, its ability to relatively broaden its functions is a *sine qua non* for its survival. Thus, its policies may have a reconciliatory tone for a long period without bearing a sustainable democratic change. Often this practice does not necessitate the establishment of the state's strong ideological (national) base.

The objectives and mechanisms that were originated or advanced by the dynamics of the nationalistic movements in the 1950s and 1960s were hijacked by the then new African nationalists, who quickly celebrated the victory of continuity in establishing neo-colonial states and promoting peripheral capitalism. The former Portuguese colonies and Sékou Touré of Guinea-Conakry were the exceptions. That is to say, many African leaders of the first generation celebrated the status quo, and therefore the sovereignty of the state did not mean structural societal change for the African masses.

Strong cooperation between the new states and the former colonial powers in trade, defense, education, finance, and technology was consolidated through dependency paradigms. This meant accepting the general rules of the international political economy and working within the framework set up by the existing dominant political philosophy of the industrial and former colonial powers. The symbol of this status quo is the pragmatic decision, made by the African heads of state in Addis Ababa in 1963, to maintain colonial boundaries.

Current events and movements have not yet fully unfolded, and they are unevenly spread across Africa. Their force depends on the dynamics of local conditions, among other factors. At this time, however, an observable level of enthusiasm among the African people, across class, gender, and religious boundaries, for promoting and supporting democracy is so high that it is unlikely that anyone or any institution will be able to stop it. It may be slowed down, or it may be weakened by factors such as corruption, military intervention, or ethnic manipulations, but it will not be halted. The word "democracy" has almost become a magical incantation, and people's expectations about what democracy could bring to their lives are enormous. Even the leftist African scholars who did not take the studies of democracy seriously in the 1960s and 1970s, and who also dismissed democracy as being associated with liberal or bourgeois thinking, are obliged to accept the fact that some kind of "people's power" is being expressed in many of the current struggles. Indeed, even in the economically poorest countries in Africa, people are demonstrating the desire to change and become part of the political process. In the long term, it is likely that some positive societal projects will come out of all these struggles.

Generally, the social sciences analyze the origin, development, and interrelation of facts as they impact on society and daily living. In most parts of Africa today, people's behavior indicates that a change is taking place in politics and society. There is an energy that must be critically studied and understood. After the failures of the development paradigms and policies in the past four decades, is there a grand social and political design taking place to deal with the resultant malaise? Who are the designers, if any? For some time, identifying what has been taking place in recent years in African political and social life has been an object of curiosity for scholars. Are we observing now in Africa democratic processes (debates that are themselves philosophically democratic), or processes of democracy (processes that can lead to democratic debates and policies), or both?

As previously mentioned, this study is guided and shaped by comparative structural-historical typologies, as they have been articulated in, and emerged from, the literature of the Third World Forum scholarship and research activities in Africa.[7] Here, social phenomena are perceived as not being structurally autonomous unto themselves. Each element of the structure of things has its own identity or property, and the whole and the parts relate to each other dynamically. Within the framework of comparative paradigms, the struggle for democracy is analyzed as a dynamic problem and not as a finite process. Thus, only broad questions and general hypotheses are raised and discussed.

These questions and hypotheses may be a response to the activities of states, political parties, civil societies, or political debates on state and state relations with society. However, democratic discourses are mainly concerned with power: how it is produced and accumulated, its social implications and ramifications, and, above all, its relationship to the control over resources. These discourse are concerned with the logic, rationality, and reality of how to govern and be governed within a given state and society, party, or any other form of political community. They express the ideas of public policies, the maintenance of the system, and the kind of political community, if any, to be promoted by a given political formation or grouping.

One of the current dominant intellectual tendencies among scholars and policymakers is to equate democratic discourses (debates, practices, and policies) and politics (for instance, freedom of expression, including free political choice, competitive politics, respect for social and human rights and laws, and the struggle for economic and cultural independence) with multipartyism; whereas dictatorship is associated with the one-party state. This raises serious epistemological and policy questions as to our definitions and understanding of what democracy is, or ought to be, in the African context. The similar tendency to equate any centralized social system with dictatorship and any decentralized social system, even one without participatory policies with democracy creates confusion about the meaning of democracy. What do the one-party state in Tanzania under Julius Nyerere and the multiparty system under Mobutu of Zaïre[8] or Paul Biya of Cameroon have in common democratically? How can one examine and define Museveni's position that Uganda should be democratic, but at the same time, it should avoid the adoption of multipartyism? Is Museveni's one party state in Uganda, with all its efforts toward reconstruction through decentralization, socially and philosophically less dynamic than multipartyism in Kenya under Moi? All these tendencies promote the notion of a restrictive democracy that may not properly reflect the demands articulated in the past few years by the new popular movements in Africa. A critical analysis of democratic discourses will shed light on the burning question of what democracy is and what it ought to be, as well as on its correlations with social policies and social progress.

While social and economic conditions in most parts of Africa are worsening, the euphoria associated with the rise of popular and democratic movements raises new expectations, hopes, and enthusiasm about the future of the new African societies. The 1995 elections in Ethiopia and Zimbabwe attracted a high level of participation and enthusiasm. Despite the militaristic approach used by General Ibrahima Babangida to establish bipartyism in Nigeria, the massive participation in the presidential elections of June 1993, which the military regime claimed to be fraudulent, reflects a high level of enthusiasm for the establishment of democracy. The decision made by 40 human organizations on August 2, 1993, to challenge Babangida's military government as it approached the return to civilian democratic rule in the country is another signal of the people's enthusiasm for the struggle for democracy. Even Chief Shoyekan's transitional government, imposed by Babangida, had the support of the traditional chiefs, including the Muslims in the North. Moreover, in the CAR, participation in the presidential election of August 1993 was spectacular. When Etienne Tshisekedi wa Mulumba was elected in Zaïre's national conference as the prime minister of the interim government on August 15, 1992, the masses rose up on the streets of Kinshasa and other cities, as if they were celebrating a new independence. The festivities took two days. Although there is no reason to doubt the basis of this hope or these high expectations, there are no economic and sociological data yet, in the African context, to support the assumptions that there are always positive correlations between the demands for democratic discourse and the level of social and economic development or progress.

Why is it that public policies, based on and defined within the framework of the multiparty democratic process or liberal democracy, are producing the worst social and economic conditions in many parts of the world, including Eastern Europe? There is no clear indication so far that programs of privatization and the dictatorship of the market promoted by both the World Bank and the IMF, both of which have been implemented within the framework of multiparty democracy, are succeeding in qualitatively transforming productive forces and substantially improving the living standard of the people in the former Soviet Union, despite significant financial aid and other economic assistance from the West for its reconstruction. Rather, there are indications of the amassing of wealth by a few entrepreneurs, as well as increasing social gaps, absolute poverty, and homelessness.[9] Is the process already too slow to bear visible fruit? In any case, as argued further in this book, democratic discourses by themselves, as articulated from the liberal perspective, do not automatically produce a higher standard of living for the majority of people. Although Russia and Africa are moving toward multipartyism, they are coming from different starting points. Can policies similar to those formulated and implemented in the countries of the former Soviet bloc produce positive results in Africa, bringing wealth and social progress?

The arguments advanced in many parts of this book show that there is no evidence to support such an assumption.

Theoretically, however, democratic discourses that are inclusive and integrative can systematically promote a diversity of views and opinions, and they can value consensus, tolerance based on law and culture, and respect for individual and collective social rights and liberties. They also are potential forces that can produce mechanisms through which social progress can occur. They can liberate minds, energize cultures, and promote individual and collective initiatives. With this theoretical basis in mind, what is the situation in Africa?

Understanding the nature of democratic discourses at a given time and in a given society (political community) requires analyzing the dynamics of state-society relations, the history of political culture, and the nature of the political regime, including its processes of self-reproduction. Historically, democratic discourses must be understood contextually: that is to say, in the context of local conditions. Functionally, their significance can be appreciated globally. Are democratic discourses and the discourses of the political opposition parties, as they interact with one another in Africa, the same thing? Must democratic discourses be culturally sensitive?

As previously indicated, since the end of the 1980s, new popular movements have been mushrooming throughout Africa, and old ones have been consolidated. Some have used violent radical means to try to achieve their ends or to publicly share their claims, while others have opted for peaceful, accommodationist approaches to advance their political agenda. The choice of the above strategies is generally based on a complex combination of factors, such as the nature of the economy and the market, and the nature of the struggle in local conditions. Generally, however, contemporary movements that have "popularistic" behavior are opportunistic in their relationship to a given defined collective agenda, but this depends on the social and political context in which the movement has operated and on its dominant ideology, if any. Recently, in Africa, some of the movements that originated and functioned as popular or social movements have succeeded in transforming themselves into legal political parties: the South West African People's Organization (SWAPO), now the ruling party in Namibia; the ANC, the ruling party in South Africa; the Movement for Justice in Africa (MOJA) in Liberia; the *Front Populaire Ivorien* (FPI) in Côte d'Ivoire; the Forum for the Restoration of Democracy (FORD) in Kenya; and the Alliance of Democratic Forces for the Liberation Congo (ADFLC), to cite only a few examples. Each of these groups with the exception of the ADFLC, fulfilled the criteria established by the government for legalization of political formations and political activities without necessarily changing their populist base.

In other political situations, within the context of pluralistic democracy, some movements are still functioning and performing their protest actions as populist movements without any concrete national political platforms. In fact, *les gens de la rue* ("the people in the street") rarely distinguish between legalized and non-legalized political groupings. Although they may know what they wish to be or what they want to acquire, generally they do not have a clear or specific idea of how to go about realizing their desires. However, both political parties and populist movements in

Africa claim, through their slogans, to pursue democratic discourses. Given the fact that the rules of their games and their actors and actresses are different in their deontology, populist movements and political parties must function in two different political spaces and under different regulations.

Populist movements have general agendas. They mobilize intentions and often transcend ideologies and ethnic and gender boundaries. Their actions also tend to have strong local or regional connotations and content. Political parties in general have specific agendas that focus on specific common interests. They transform ideas and desires into manageable proposals. Their proposals are generally ideologically defined. While some parties are highly influenced by foreign powers, and such parties usually have legalistic tendencies, in action, political parties and populist movements complement each other.

NOTES

1. Michael Bratton, "Are Competitive Elections Enough?," *Africa Demos* 3: 4 (March 1995): 7.

2. Jacques Mariel Nzouankeu, "The Role of the National Conference in the Transition to Democracy in Africa: The Cases of Bénin and Mali," *Issue: A Journal of Opinion*, 21:1–2 (1993): 44.

3. To borrow Immanuel Wallerstein's definition, an antinomy between state and society involves a permanent tension, a permanent disequilibrium. *The World Politics of the World Economy: The States, the Movements and the Civilizations* (New York: Cambridge University Press, 1984), p. 175.

4. Nii K. Bentsi-Enchill, "Modest Economic Upturn," *Africa Recovery*, 8: 3 (December 1994), 13.

5. Issa Shivji, "The POs and the NGOs: Reflections on the Place of the Working People in the Battle for Democracy," *CODESRIA Bulletin* 4 (1990): 9.

6. In the 1960s and early 1970s, the study of democracy in developing countries was dominated by various modernization theorists, such as Samuel Huntington, E. David Apter, Gabriel Almond, and Joseph LaPalombra. African scholars, especially the leftists, were mainly interested in political economic studies, as eloquently reflected in the works of Claude Ake, Samir Amin, and Ibbo Mandaza. Studies on democracy were conceived as a *prolongement* ("prolongation") of liberal scholarship and philosophy: bourgeois studies were considered ahistorical and reactionary. This situation has changed intellectually because of the current changes in world politics and the African crisis.

7. The Third World Forum has developed out of research centers in Africa, especially UNITAR in Dakar, to contribute to the understanding of social phenomena from a Third World perspective. This is represented by organic intellectuals such as Samir Amin, as *le chef de fil* (leader), and the late Claude Ake, who argue that, though a dependency theory can provide a universal or international explanation of the causes and structures of underdevelopment in Africa, the dynamics of local conditions, such as culture and class, must be taken seriously as part of the objective conditions. There is an intellectual tendency here to go beyond the satellite relations with the metropolis and their paradigms to see the local and regional objective conditions as essentially dynamic.

8. On May 16, 1997, after capturing Kinshasa (the capital city) and chasing Joseph-Désiré Mobutu Sese Seko out of the office that he took by a military *"coup d'état"* on

November 24, 1965, Laurent-Désiré Kabila, the leader of the Alliance of Democratic Forces for the Liberation of the Congo (ADFLC), declared himself president of the country and officially changed the name of Zaïre to the Democratic Republic of Congo. He formed a union government on May 22, 1997. Thus, this book uses the name "Zaïre" when specifically analyzing the regime of Mobutu; however, to indicate other periods, it uses "Congo" or the "Democratic Republic of Congo." To be able to depict history accurately, Zaïre and the Congo are used interchangeably depending on the context.

9. For further information on the economic conditions in the former Soviet Union and Eastern Europe, see the well-written article by John H. Mutti, "Economic Policy and Democratization in the Former Communist States," in *Democratic Theory and Post-Communist Change*, ed. Robert D. Grey (Upper Saddle River, NJ: Prentice Hall, 1997), pp. 217–247.

2

The Nature of Democratic Discourses in the 1990s

Two major schools of thought have emerged from the pragmatic activities of current popular movements and the various strategies that have been used by different social classes and political parties to capture state power in Africa. Some people and members of political parties believe that the issues, processes, and forms of democracy and society to be created and established in Africa must be first debated in a national forum, a national conference. Bénin was the vanguard in the evolution of this thought, but there the state was highly involved in organizing the conference. The national conference has been perceived by many members of the opposition parties as sovereign and independent of the state's activities, policies, and structures. Some leaders of the political opposition, like Francis Wodié,[1] of the *Parti Ivorien du Travail* (PIT) in Côte d'Ivoire, believe that an African state is an illegitimate political entity to organize elections or to create the rules for the transition to democracy. He believes that *"La liberté du pluralisme est antithétique au monopartisme et parti-État"* (liberty of multipartyism is antithetical to monopartyism and party-state). Multipartyism cannot function on the rules and logic of the one-party state, be it civilian or military. The existing state is not ontologically capable of producing the rules that can promote multipartyism or democracy because its philosophical base is antithetical to the democratic foundation. The state cannot defeat its raison d'être. From this perspective, democracy is first of all a national issue. The choice of the form of democracy must be publicly debated by representatives from various social formations and the civil society. In countries like Bénin (the leader of this movement), the Central African Republic, Chad, the Congo, Gabon, Madagascar, Niger, Togo, and the Democratic Republic of Congo, the option of public debate was strongly considered by the opposition parties as the best way to start national debate on the democratization process and development issues.

On the other hand, there are others who believe that pressuring the state to initiate major political reforms may also advance the cause of democracy through peaceful means, that is to say, through debates leading to consensus. Here the initiatives to set up democratic processes and all the rules of the game must come from the state, which has to accept the principle of political reforms and power sharing with the opposition parties at some stage or relinquish power to the opposition leaders if they are elected. The state has the reason and will to promote change. For instance, in Bénin, the government of Mathieu Kérékou convened a national conference on February 19, 1990 in Cotonou. The state's survival depends on its ability to adapt to the conditions of change. For different reasons, Moi of Kenya, for example, believes in the interventionism of the state. Although his party has had more seats in the national assembly than any single opposition party, Moi was re-elected in the December 1992 (and also in December 1997) elections without necessarily winning the elections. He literally bought the elections. Thus, he is ruling the country without a strong, supportive national consensus. More important is the involvement of the state in creating mechanisms to establish new democratic rules. For example, despite protests over this method, Jerry Rawlings in Ghana initiated democratic reforms from below, and even Ibrahim Babangida in Nigeria imposed a two-party political system model from the top, which legalized both the National Republican Convention (NRC) and the Social Democratic Party (SDP). The process that Babangida created has not been democratic for Nigeria.

Frederick de Klerk in South Africa, in a limited way, also fits in this category (state's interventionism) although the African National Congress (ANC), formerly a major social movement and now a political party, and other democratic organizations, have continuously succeeded in forcibly intervening in the agenda of state political reforms and procedures. As Hermann Giomee stated:

South Africa has long been considered one of the countries where a transition to democracy is least likely. Yet in the beginning of 1990 the ruling National Party (NP) did the unthinkable: it deliberately embarked on a process that would end white rule.[2]

However, without the ANC's strong intervention, no significant political reforms would be implemented in South Africa. Although the state may not have undertaken the political reforms in good conscience, it accepted the idea that they should be pursued. The political debate here took the form of a prolonged national conference.

Félix Houphouët-Boigny of Côte d'Ivoire also believed that state political reforms could lead to the advancement of multiparty democratic discourses. Shortly before his death in December 1993, he insisted that everything was possible or negotiable in Côte d'Ivoire and that democracy should come peacefully and in an orderly fashion. Of course, peace and order were defined not from the people's but from the state's point of view: the condition of functioning stability and maintenance of political and administrative institutions. In some countries, like Mali, opposition committees were formed through pressure from popular movements. Coalitions of various organizations led to successful presidential and legislative elections.

The success of political elections by itself does not necessarily mean the establishment of democracy, but rather a process that can lead to the establishment of democracy. One of the working assumptions of this book is that countries such as Burkina Faso, Bénin, and the Sudan, where strong traditions of political debates (or public theaters) existed prior to the emergence of the current movements, are more likely to succeed in establishing mechanisms of liberal democratic discourses than countries where a multiparty system was imposed, artificially accommodated (Lumumba-Kasongo, 1991a), or came as a surprise. For example, Cameroon and Côte d'Ivoire established what can be characterized as "multiparty autocracies:" systems that were almost totally controlled by the state and the ruling party. Paul Biya and Félix Houphouët-Boigny refused to support the idea of establishing a sovereign national conference. After elections, the government and the ruling party have tried to limit an openness and the debates that are associated with liberal multipartyism. This has been the case in Egypt for many years. As will be further analyzed, multiparty autocracy cannot function properly in today's Kenya and Nigeria. Although the opposition parties did not build a consensus to effectively challenge Moi of Kenya in the presidential elections in early 1993, they were relatively well represented in the Kenyan parliament. Here national issues were critically debated even with the domination of the ruling party, the Kenya African National Union (KANU). To a large extent, this has not been the case in Côte d'Ivoire (until recently) and Cameroon.

In short, despite the fact that the history of political formation, political culture, and the style of governance in Côte d'Ivoire and Cameroon are different, towards the 1980s, both Félix Houphouët-Boigny and Paul Biya produced "autocratic multipartyism." While Cameroon has not decided to break away from this style yet, in Côte d'Ivoire, especially after the passing of Houphouët-Boigny, the new pluralistic politics is gradually weakening the foundation of "autocratic multipartyism." The media has become more open and the opposition political expression is relatively tolerated by the ruling party (PDCI). The idea of sharing power is not as distant as it used to be during Houphouët-Boigny's era. In Cameroon, Paul Biya was re-elected in 1997 without changing his style of governance.

Will a "multiparty autocracy" last a long time, given both the level of economic malaise and the level of organization of the opposition parties? In Ghana, opposition parties boycotted the legislative elections of early 1993. How much have they accomplished as extra-parliamentarian oppositions? Although oppositions have been operating out of the assembly, they have been properly using the court system to challenge the ruling party. Democratic structures allow this kind of mechanism to be used by the opposition parties or any citizen who disagrees with state policies.

As stated earlier, African societies are in a hybrid, fragile transition that may easily shift to either the establishment of some form of democracy or a return to dictatorship. The initial political, social, and economic conditions and the existing political culture determine how societies will be organized and governed through this transition. This should in principle be considered a movement away from dictatorship, totalitarianism, tyranny, and the one-party state to multiparty politics and democracy, and from one form of government or regime to another. If the elements of change and their political foundations, if any, are not embodied in the process of creating this transition, political and economic progress will not be possible. Although this may be a caricature of reality, it is certain that Africa is in transition.

The nature of this transition depends on how the institutions of democracy are established, how the whole democratic process started, how states are dealing with the economic crisis, and above all, the nature of initial conditions. Of course, at this time, any attempt to maintain or restore dictatorship in most countries will be met with resistance, given the increase in the people's political consciousness as reflected by current social movements. Political consciousness is an expression of people's collective awareness of the significance of political events at the national level. However, the nature of the power struggle between a particular people and its ruling classes depends on their political culture and social conditions. In addition to internal and national factors, the nature of the relationship between a given ruling class and foreign powers may determine the kind of struggle that will take place in a society. There are no signs at present that any form of democracy is firmly winning ground in the continent, even in cases where the old dictators have been voted out. Even Senegal, which has enjoyed for the past 15 years or so a state of multiparty politics, has gone through a serious power struggle that is undermining the strength of liberal democratic principles. In addition, the impact of the Structural Adjustment Programs (SAPs) of the World Bank and the International Monetary Fund (IMF) and their unpopular policies, which are based on austerity programs on the job market and public spending are working against liberal democracy and the people's initiatives. The time for celebrating democracy has not come yet. Perhaps it is too soon and therefore incorrect at this juncture of history to talk in terms of celebration.

The establishment of any form of democracy will depend on the effort of the conscious social classes, their organizations, and committed African leaders to bring their skills, expertise and experience into praxis to make hard policy choices and cooperate with one another to improve the social, economic, and political environment for the majority of people. For democracy to be in motion in Africa, ballots and food staples must come at the same time. One without the other will lead to illusions, unfulfilled and broken hopes, and ultimately to violence. The question of youth employment, which is vital for the national economy, must also be tackled democratically. The most important point is that democracy without a philosophical basis cannot embody the societal projects that Africans at this point demand. It is not the level of economic development or growth that will determine the success of the democratic struggle in Africa. Rather, the degree of political consciousness of the various classes and their interactions with the economic actors is more likely to be the major factor. Finally, do democratic discourses in the transitional Africa have philosophical bases? What is the sociological impact of these discourses?

This book argues that democratic discourses have an integral local and universal philosophical significance: All rational human beings (and all human beings are rational when it comes to their wants, desires, and interests) aspire to be happy in their social milieux and eagerly participate in the process of organizing their societies and their reproduction according to chosen norms. The forms that such participation or self-realization can take are not and cannot be similar. Local expressions of democratic discourse take different forms and voices because of local cultural, historical, and social class peculiarities. Thus, democratic discourses may mean different things for different constituencies, audiences, and classes. However, most current popular movements in Africa claim to be democratic in some way.

As reflected in the agenda of many current popular movements, claims for advancing democratic discourses have been articulated and actualized through protests against political establishments: the ruling parties (and their domestic and national policies) and their allies, some of which have ruled alone or in a coalition of other social groups (clientism) for some time. Those ruling parties have resisted any fundamental change on the basis of their historical legacy. For instance, in Zaïre, Togo, and Zambia, Mobutu, Eyadema, and Kaunda (the former president of Zambia) each claimed to be the founder of his respective post-colonial state. Unlike Mobutu, Kaunda accepted defeat in the presidential elections of 1991, although he indicated in early 1994 that he would compete again for the presidential elections if economic and social conditions continue to deteriorate or if the level of governmental corruption goes up. Most of these leaders intended to create states before forming nations. In Côte d'Ivoire, for example, President Félix Houphouët-Boigny ruled the country from the time he was a legislator in the French parliament in the 1940s until his death in December 1993. He once said to the protesting *Ivoriens* students in 1960, *"Je vous ai fait sortir du trou"* ("I brought you out of the depths"). In this case, the basis of his legitimacy was historical.

Protest movements personally targeted heads of state or presidents, regardless of their real or fictitious accomplishments, but not necessarily the philosophical or ideological base of their regimes. However, there are some exceptions. For instance, in Mali and, to a certain extent in Togo, Moussa Traoré's regime, as well as that of Eyadema, were targeted. In Ghana, Rawlings's regime was targeted by the opposition parties as well, not necessarily on the basis of its performance, but because it was a military regime. However, this military regime was different from other ones. Rawlings had a national development agenda for the rural population. In most cases, from the activism of populist movements (which generally kept their popularistic character after becoming political parties), emerged the idea of the national conference as the most important medium for democratic discourse.

National conferences, mostly financed and supported by Western donors, especially France, Germany, and the United States, took place in many parts of Africa without any prior serious and systematic consultation with the masses. For example, in Bénin, the Congo, Mali, Niger, Togo, and South Africa, national conferences operated within a formal and informal framework at the same time. Enthusiasm and spontaneity characterized the behaviour of the participants. In some cases, these two phenomena did not lead to a concise elaboration of the programs. The Convention of Democratic South Africa (CODESA) was confronted with a more challenging task because of the nature of the conflict to be solved in South Africa. Despite local and national differences in the way national conferences operated, they commonly articulated the guidelines for the establishment of transitional governments, the preparations for legislative and presidential elections, and the promotion of multipartyism. It was assumed by the participants, who represented almost every large segment of society, that multipartyism with its constitutional base would promote democratic discourses, particularly concerning issues related to public policy debates, which include social equality, justice, freedom, employment, distribution of resources, regional development, and the well-being of the individual and society at large.

National conferences have been perceived and acted upon as sovereign organs of society and have become veritable citadels of the opposition parties against the states, especially the heads of state. In African politics, states are identified or fused with the heads of state. For instance, Etienne Gnasingbé Eyadema (president of Togo), Dénis Sassou Nguesso (former president of the Republic of Congo, but he recaptured power by military means in 1997), and Mathieu Kérékou (former president of Bénin and reelected in 1996) were left, through the resolutions of the national conferences held before the presidential elections, without any real executive or military power. Although Eyadema is still in office and succeeded in becoming once again part of the multiparty democratic process, the situation in Togo is not different from that of other African states, concerning the mission of the national conference. However, what should be carefully studied is how, before the August 1993 presidential elections, Eyadema and Koffigoh (then the leaders of the opposition) found themselves on the same political spectrum after a bitter power struggle. How, did Koffigoh become Eyadema's protégé? The response can be found in the nature of the relations of power within the opposition parties and the relations between them and the state.

In other cases, like Zaïre, the process of creating a functioning and productive national forum faced massive obstructions created by Mobutu, who was more determined than any other African president to destroy it. The national conference was paralyzed for more than six months by Mobutu's criminal actions in 1992. The opposition parties, especially the *Union Sacrée* (US),[3] firmly believed that the national conference was a legitimate exercise that could peacefully open avenues for political change in the country. However, with Mobutu as the head of state and commander-in-chief of the army, even if he could govern without "reigning," the chance of having a normal and successful national debate in Zaïre was remote. Though the compromise of maintaining Mobutu as the president in the transitional government was strategically realistic with the support of the United States government, it was a bad test of a democratic compromise. He ruled the country for almost 32 years like his own real estate, a Leopoldian model. From a Machiavellian point of view, Mobutu did not have any real reason to be moral or to promote democracy through a genuine national conference. He amassed wealth— the basis of his political actions. On this basis, until the time he was forced to flee the country on May 15, 1997, he created a successful client regime.

Generally, the national conference, as it publicized its democratic slogans and projected possibilities for the success of a democratic society, did not play the role of a serious political educator. It was a more or less legal authority established by both the state and the opposition parties with a special mission to develop and set up general rules and conditions in which potential democratic discourses could take place; it was a stage in the process of democratic debates. It is up to the transitional governments, civil societies, political parties, and organized masses to undertake the task of setting democratic discourses in motion. An important question is: In cases where parties have decided only to articulate and advance their goals through a power struggle rather than an ideological struggle, who should be the political educator? Who should educate or socialize the people about democracy? What kind of democracy is relevant to African conditions?

Democracy, as conceived by the national conferences in most parts of Africa, has generally become synonymous with multipartyism. Debates about both delegative and representative democracies occur at these conferences. One common recommendation of national conferences has been that transitional governments, whose prime ministers have to be elected by conference participants, should organize legislative and presidential elections based on the liberal constitutional model. Thus, liberal democracy is considered and adopted into the political process and policy as the only functioning model of democracy. The technical, rigorous procedures and legalism of this type of democracy, as reflected, for instance, in the U.S. Constitution, rather than its substance, are becoming the most important features of African constitutionalism. Yet, for this constitutionalism to effectively work, citizens must be well informed about its potentialities and how it could effectively function. People must know their rights before they can exercise them. They must know the limits of those rights by law. In most countries, the new constitution was approved without a national referendum. It was probably assumed that the constituencies represented in the national conference had a broad base, and that therefore their views reflected the views of the majority of the people. In most cases there were no systematic debates on the kind of society that should be built in Africa. A similar mistake was committed by many nationalists in the 1950s and 1960s when Western parliamentarian systems, without any rigorous debates and people's participation, were adopted as the political model of governance. The masses, who are the majority and live in rural areas, had hardly any opportunity to define what democracy is or ought to be for them. Once again the so-called philosopher-kings and the prophets of the new movements believed they knew what is or ought to be good for all. This concept needs to be critically debated within the framework of the struggle for democracy in Africa.

From a social theory perspective, the apparent victory of liberal constitutionalism, in a world that in reality is culturally and philosophically polycentric, is an epistemological problem. Polycentrism, as manifested in local, national, and regional movements, has not been translated into policies and development models, nor have its advocates clearly and consistently elaborated its economic assumptions in any region of the world. The so-called victory of the liberal democracy and the international capitalism has been the product of the combined activities of popular movements and of national conferences wherever they took place in Africa, power struggles among the opposition parties, the collapse of peripheral capitalism, and external factors. As mentioned earlier, most national conferences were sponsored and provided with financial assistance by Europe and the United States. What are the implications of such a sponsorship for an activity that was supposed to be essentially national? Can it be neutral? Did it shape the content of the debates and their outcomes? What does the sponsorship mean in terms of political and social implications? Is it also purely a coincidence that several prime ministers (or their cabinet directors) or other prominent ministers, who have emerged out of the activities of national conferences, are associated with the IMF or the World Bank technocracy? Is there any reason to be suspicious about the national conference process?

This is not the first time that liberal democracy or multipartyism has been tried in Africa. Although the conditions that led to the rise of multipartyism in the past are not fully examined within this book, it is clear that at the end of the 1950s and the early 1960s this phenomenon emerged in almost every corner of Africa where there were struggles for political independence. Parliamentary democracy was *à la mode* ("fashionable") then. For instance, between October 1946, which is the birth date of the *Rassemblement Démocratique Africain* (RDA) led by Félix Houphouët-Boigny, and 1959, the birth date of the *Parti de la Fédération Africaine* (PFA) of Léopold Senghor and Modibo Keita, there were more than 30 active political parties in French West Africa alone (Harshé, 1984, 146–147). During the Cold War, however, the major actors and their ideologies did not allow these struggles to operate freely. Because of the multitude of external and internal constraints and interventions, and the impact of the Cold War, among other factors, the movement towards multipartyism was doomed to fail. It was hijacked by the then-emerging African petty bourgeoisie, who had a special role to play in the "worldization" of African politics and its European partners. That is to say that the politics of the African bourgeoisie and those of their European sponsors led to worldize African politics. That role was to maintain the status quo.

At the national as well as the global level, the context in which the new multipartyism has emerged is qualitatively different from that of the years of struggle for political independence. The worsening of African social and economic conditions, the end of the Cold War, the re-emergence of Americanism that occurred after World War II, the effort to practically realize the unification of Western Europe, the rise of Islamic fundamentalism, the globalization of industrial and transnational capitals, and the activism of grassroots movements in Africa, to cite only a few factors, make this era different from the 1950s and 1960s. The politics and policies of integrating Africa into the world system have become relatively stable.

To understand the political and intellectual context in which democracy is being articulated, it is important to first define democracy in a broad theoretical framework and discuss its historical impact in a contemporary African context. Has Africa inherited some democratic traditions from the West?

As already discussed, parliamentarianism was tried in the 1960s, though for a short period of time in many cases. Leaders like Kofi Abrefa Busia of Ghana and Nnandi Azikiwe of Nigeria firmly believed that liberal parliamentarianism was the way to state- and nation-building. In terms of its potential performance, it was perceived to be superior to other forms of governance. However, toward the end of the 1960s, the results of experiments with this form of democracy in Africa were not positive. Dealing with this issue requires a brief discussion of Western political thought, especially in its relationship to democracy.

In inventing Eurocentrism as an ideology, during the Renaissance, the European elite, kings, high priests, and local feudal powers decided through armed struggles, treaties, congresses, and the mission of the Roman Catholic church to create a common cultural and philosophical foundation for the development of their ideals and ambitions. Through this construct, at the beginning of the 15th century, the ideas of the European democracies became intellectually, though not historically or linguistically, linked with Greek civilization. The Holy Roman Empire provided a unified cultural basis for this construct. European Greek philosophers, such as Aristotle, Plato, and Socrates (who were considered democrats at the time, but would not be considered so by contemporary standard), defined democracy as the right of citizens to participate in the affairs of the *polis* ("city-state"). These rights were considered inalienable because they were conceived to be naturally rooted in the biology of society. Democracy was defined as the right to acquire power and property without necessarily social struggle or the individual hard work ethic (meritocracy) of Max Weber. In a broad context, its outcome, implications, and processes could not be evaluated in moral or individual terms. The same thing was true in caste societies in many parts of the world, including Africa and Asia. In general, however, despite its exclusiveness, democracy was perceived by the Greeks to be a government of the people, for the people, and by the people.[4] Jean-Jacques Rousseau became the incarnation of this principle in France and in all of Europe. Rousseau philosophized about democracy and universalized it as a social theory.

Who are the people (*demos*) in this context? Despite the multitude of cultures and social systems in pre-colonial Africa, generally "people" meant a community of cultures and not necessarily a community of interests in the technical sense. Property, which was (and still is in many ways) associated in the West with *demos* and citizenry had a communitarian value in Africa. Here generally property is a socially defined rather than an individually owned phenomenon. Democracy is not a general social term or behavior. In ancient Greek society, it had a biological character with social ramifications. It was a system for an enlightened few. Women, slaves, merchants, and strangers could not by their own intelligence or hard work (merits) become "people." Women, for instance, were considered "natural accidents." They could not own any property with political significance. The amount of property (for instance, slaves and land) that one had, reflected the amount power that one could exercise. One could not inherit the title "people." The peripheral classes (the non people group) in the Greek classification could contribute to the state economically as controlled subjects through their labor and taxes but were not entitled to participate in political discourse, the highest expression of being citizens.

Democratic discourse was cultivated through the rigorous education of citizens. Through an elitist education, the biological disposition (embodiment of inherited individual and physical characteristics) was transformed into the social and political sphere. According to the ancient Greek philosophy, the formation of mind and physics, the two struggling entities, has a common origin. The right of citizens was ahistorical in that it did not define society in terms of its permanency of struggles for change.

In a dialectical understanding of history, social and political rights are formulated and acquired through struggle. A right like property is not just given; it is, rather, acquired. Through the struggles between church and state in medieval times and throughout the European Renaissance, and through the struggles between kings, subjects, lords, and vassals, as well as through the middle class or bourgeois revolutions—for instance, the American Revolution of 1776, the French Revolution of 1789, and the industrial revolution in England—"divine rights" were transformed into individual rights. A new ethic of individualism and its meritocratic philosophy emerged. The contract theorists universalized those rights by articulating *la sainteté du logos* (" the sacredness of the word"), which makes human beings rational and social. Later, both liberals and rationalists believed that these rights are similar, but not identical to the law of economics, the so-called natural law.

Despite social contradictions that are essentially outcomes of the history of struggles of *le rapport des forces* ("the relationship of forces") in the United States, for instance, the constitutional rights of individual citizens, guaranteed by the Bill of Rights, dynamize the United States as a political community and help keep it together. Without these (defined here as divine) rights and the mechanisms for their protection, given the level of social gaps between the haves and have-nots, the permanency of racial and ethnic tensions and social division, and the hegemonic control over the means of production by a few, the rule of accountability and other ingredients of the U.S. democracy (for instance, value and ideological consensus, and compromise),[5] would not have been strong enough to maintain political stability and the strength and pace of industrialization that the United States has enjoyed in the past 200 years or so. At a high level of political discourse and policy analysis in the 20th century, the U.S. democracy is managed by a few top members of the elite representing corporate interests. Its representative democracy can still function even without the participation of the majority. In principle, political parties were meant to contribute to cohesive policies, coherent programs, and collective accountability. Alvin So summarizes the U.S. democracy in these terms:

Democracy, in Lipset's work, refers to a political system that supplies regular constitutional opportunities for changing the governing officials, and that permits the population to influence major decisions by choosing the holders of political office. (1990, 49)

In addition to accountability, which is the major factor regulating the relations and behavior between the elected and electors in Western societies, the attributes of democracy include an open political competition and electoral pluralism, which also characterize the liberal approach to the market and its forces. It is a system in which the majority of interests are in rough equilibrium, a system through which the leaders must compete for the support of the members, and a system in which constitutional guarantees of basic freedom are actually in force.[6]

Representative democracy (or *le système démocratique parlementaire*) in the West has succeeded to guarantee in theory the rights of both the state and individual citizens, through respect of the law, and the authority and values of the constitution. In a multiparty government, including the United States with its government that is constitutionally multiparty but biparty in practice,[7] the party is not identical to the state. Electoral codes are not identical to the Bill of Rights. States can use party ideologies for advancing the interests of the elite. This should, in general, be guided by some constitutional framework. There is a separation between the state and party in their *démarche politique* ("political action"). In principle, all parties are equal in the face of the constitution. Interests of the parties, including those of the ruling parties, are not necessarily similar or identical to those of the state.

Since the 1980s, for instance, the socialist party in France has never behaved as a member of the international socialist organization to which it had a commitment in foreign and military policies for developing countries. François Mitterand promised the end of capitalism in France with its contradictions, whatever that means. However, the interests of France as a nation prevailed. In 1993 the constitutional marriage between François Mitterand and Edouard Baladure, the French conservative prime minister, reflected the complex role of political party and state in a parliamentary system. The socialist president was obliged by the law of the land to work with the conservatives (a coalition government), who became the majority party as a result of winning the parliamentarian elections. Parties behave differently because of their different political histories, ideologies, and relations to the dominant social groups, and the dominant political culture of society at large.

However, parties in power (ruling parties) do have the leverage to manipulate or use power relations for their own advantage to acquire more resources or support for their programs. No party permanently has special relations with the state. Regarding the role of the opposition party, in Europe, for example, the difference between the parties is mostly ideological (or normative guideline) or substantial (referring to political and social policy). The opposition parties often try to bring their agenda to the government based on their ideological positions. In the United States, for instance, the ideological differences between the two political parties are not significant. To a certain extent, the role of the opposition party here seems to be similar to its role in Europe; however, in Europe the ideological differences between parties make its political pluralism more challenging. Theodore Lowi discusses this issue by stating that:

The fundamental requirement of accountability is a two-party system in which the opposition party acts as critic. . . . presenting the policy alternatives that are necessary for a true choice in reaching public decisions.[8]

The opposition parties are supposed to challenge the ruling parties on the issues of public policies, state security, and the citizens' welfare. This can be done effectively if the rules of the game are well-defined and the parties involved in the process of governance know their legal function as stipulated by the constitution. How have the above elements of democratic discourse in the West been incorporated in colonial and post-colonial politics in Africa?

As previously discussed, colonial political experiences were essentially undemocratic and militaristic. Democracy and imperialism probably do have many relations between them, especially as they manifest themselves in a colonial context, but theoretically they cannot and do not positively complement each other. Colonies were administered with iron rules, whose implementation and impact varied from one region to another depending on the degree of local resistance and politics, and the quality and quantity of available resources.

Contemporary democratic discourses in Africa rose from the dynamics of popular movements, international power struggles, and colonial state reforms. African nationalists inherited the concept of the right to self-determination, which in fact is the right of the state to rule. This notion of self-determination was also developed out of the discourses of the international system of states namely, the League of Nations and the United Nations. The right of self-determination is the right of self-governance. This right is not the same as the right of the individual or society at large to freely participate in the political affairs of the state and society, or the right to be equally protected by the law. The Houphouët-Boignys, the Kenyattas, the Kaundas, the Lumumbas, and the Nkrumahs, had some notions of democratic rights in their agendas as they fought for self-determination. Their main objective, however, was to struggle or negotiate for political independence. Political independence, as a right of a nation-state, does not automatically lead to an individual or collective democratic right. The historical context in which nationalists operated in the 1950s and 1960s was dominated by the supremacy of the statist right. By this logic, the state should have a right to exist for its own sake. How do statist rights, rights to self-determination, expand or transform themselves into individual or social human rights? This was the role that each constitution in each country was supposed to perform after independence. How well did it perform?

African post-colonial political experiences reflect a diversity of approaches to the function and maintenance of state sovereignty. The Modernization school of thought believed that the establishment of strong states could pave the way to development. Why is it that all African-Marxist, African-socialist, liberal, and military regimes ended up establishing a one-party state? Was the party-state model of articulating state affairs imposed or chosen by the new political elite? Was a one-party state necessarily or ontologically anti-democratic? Was it the outcome of an international conspiracy or a deliberate choice by some nationalists to protect their own power by not allowing any political challenge? The issue is complex. However, Peter Anyang' Nyong'o is correct as he said:

It would, perhaps, be historically incorrect to argue that the first advocates of "one party democracy" had, from the very beginning, a hidden agenda for authoritarianism. Authoritarianism perhaps emerged historically as the post-colonial state was faced with competing demands for scarce resources; it is only those who could be processed into outputs without disrupting the system were allowed in through the political sluice gates of authoritarian governance.[9]

The majority of the African political elite of the first generation simultaneously inherited the values of dictatorship and those of liberal democracy. Many British colonies, such as Ghana, Nigeria, and the Sudan, were prepared for constitutional rule. But after African countries earned independence, with the exception of a few countries (the Gambia, Senegal, the Sudan, Ghana, and Nigeria in limited periods, and Egypt in limited ways), multipartyism was, until recently, generally perceived as taboo institutionally and structurally. The main preoccupation was to try to maintain national unity. In many cases, democratic discourses, which include the right to basic liberties, for instance, of religion, of movement, and of speech, practically did not exist. To establish the basis for a theoretical generalization about the nature of these discourses and to raise further questions as to their relevance in the current situation in Africa, the following paragraph discusses the assumptions behind the concept of democracy. An important assumption about democracy is that all rational human beings aspire to have some form of democratic rights, including the right to life in their own social milieu. The basis for this reasoning is both philosophical and biological. Those rights are fundamental for the progress and survival of human beings. This general categorization is ethically universal. Democracy is an ideal political system to reach a higher societal objective because it can liberate the spirit, provide possibilities, and open up choices, and it can also protect people from the contradictions of human nature à la Hobbes. Thomas Hobbes believed that human nature is essentially in the state of anarchy. In the state of nature, human beings are constantly fighting one another. As Leon Baradat said:

Hobbes's view of people is not a happy one. He thought that people were basically self-serving. Although they were rational, they were not in control of their destinies because they were driven by an overwhelming fear of death. (1994, 64)

Pre-colonial Africa had its own democratic possibilities. Even when multipartyism *à l'Européenne* was not part of the African governance, democracy was not foreign in political structures of many communities. Democratic rights were essentially communitarian. Debates under the baobab tree in many West African regions, for example, were open until the council of elders reached consensus on the issues discussed. The Ashanti-Asante (Obeng, 1986), the Baoulé, the Bakongo, the Masai, the Tetela, the Yoruba, and the Vaï, to cite only a few examples, had their own democratic practices. Claude Ake defined democracy in these terms:

Africans have a communal consciousness; we do not think of ourselves as atomized in competition and potential conflict with others, but as members of an organic whole. African traditional democracy lies in a commitment to the desirability and necessity of participation as a collective enterprise. In the African tradition, participation does not merely enjoy rights, but secures tangible benefits. It entails active involvement in the process of deciding on common goals and how to realize them.[10]

How he arrived at such a definition is not clear, but the logic of his thinking can be historically and sociologically appreciated. How can democracy be popularized and operationalized to contribute to the development or industrialization of the continent? Salim Ahmed Salim of the Organization of African Unity (OAU) has defined democracy as

a fundamental right, an engine of liberation and catalytic agent of human development. But it is not a revelation. How it is expressed, how it is given concrete form, of necessity varies from society to society. Consequently, one should avoid the temptation of decreeing a so-called perfect model of democracy and exporting it wholesale or imposing it on another society.[11]

A discussion of the author's perspective on democracy may clarify many aspects of the arguments in this section. Democracy is not a menu prepared from the outside of a given culture. It is a political means through which social contradictions, with respect to collective and individual rights, should be solved at a given time and in a given society. There cannot be real democracy if a concerned society does not have any consciousness of its own contradictions, does not allow political debate, and does not outline a social practice to provide rules for the society to manage its interests and objectives with equity and justice. Democracy should be a struggle against social inequality, injustices, exploitation, and social miseries. That is to say, democracy is more than formal political pluralism or the process of producing an electoral code or an electoral commission. In the past, many African states produced liberal constitutions without liberal democracy or any form of democracy. Democracy is both a process and a practice that involves equal economic and social opportunities for the citizenry. It is a corrective process in which a given society, especially a formerly colonized society, is born again. Born again is used in this context as a process of reconstruction. It is a ritual processing of new ideas and policies in a given society.

This definition of democracy puts more emphasis on substance than on procedures. In short, democratic discourses must promote the values embodied in this statement, *"Tous les hommes naissent libres et sont égaux en droits"* (sic) ("All men are born free and are equal in the face of the law"). Without this basic principle, democracy can hardly be realized. This does not mean that people are identical in their outlook, interests, talents, or cultures. Acceptance and respect for differences are vital in democratic practices. The forms that democracy takes must vary from country to country and from one culture to another. Philosophically, however, the ultimate end of a democratic process should embody universalistic characteristics. That is to say, the language in which the chart of democracy is written, and how and when it is written, may differ, but the end is the collective well-being of a given society. As Michael Parenti said:

When people unite against the abuses of wealth and privilege, when they activate themselves and militantly attack the hypocrisy and lies of powers that be, when they fight back and become the active agents of their destiny, when they withdraw their empowering responses and refuse to toe that line, I have another name for that. I call it democracy.[12]

Many aspects of the popular struggle for democracy in Africa resemble Parenti's perception and definition.

NOTES

1. On August 17, 1992, the author had an intensive discussion with Professor Francis Wodié at his residence in Cocody, Abidjan. He is the General Secretary of the *Parti Ivoirien du Travail* (PIT). He is also professor in the Faculty of Law at the Université de Cocody, formerly the Université d'Abidjan, known also as *Université Nationale de* Côte d'Ivoire.

2. Hermann Giomee, "Democracy in South Africa," *Political Science Quarterly* 110:1 (Spring 1995): 83.

3. *Union Sacrée* is a coalition of political interests that operates from a vague ideological position. The common objective was originally to see Mobutu out of power. However, many elements of this union articulated the necessity for negotiating with Mobutu. In fact, many members of the Union have re-joined Mobutu's party.

4. For further information about the people as a social category, see Plato's *Republic*.

5. William W. Boyer, "Reflections on Democratization," *PS: Political Science and Politics* (September 1992): 517–20.

6. For further information on this subject, see Tukumbi Lumumba-Kasongo, *Nationalistic Ideologies, Their Policy Implications and The Struggle for Democracy in African Politics*, Lewiston, New York: Edwin Mellen Press, 1991.

7. The current movement in the United States led by the millionaire Perot to create a third political party seems to have a national momentum as the party tries to compete in the presidential elections in November 1996.

8. Theodore Lowi, "Presidential Power: Restoring the Balance," in *President, Elections and Democracy*, ed. Richard M. Pious (New York, The Academy of Political Science, 1992), p. 17.

9. Peter Anyang' Nyong'o, "Discourses on Democracy in Africa." Paper read at the Seventh General Assembly of CODESRIA, Dakar, Senegal (10–14 February 1992).

10. Claude Ake, "Democracy and Development," *West Africa* (April 1990): 49.

11. Salim Ahmed Salim, "Link National, International Democratization: OAU's Salim," *Africa Recovery* 4 (July–September 1990): 29.

12. Michael Parenti, "Fascism: The False Revolution" (Lecture given on the Alternative Radio, Berkeley, California, on 23 September, 1995), p. 7.

3

The Opposition Political Parties and Their Discourses

INTRODUCTION: ISSUES AND OBJECTIVES

The opposition political party is an essential structural characteristic of contemporary liberal democracy that has been globalized. For better or worse, all liberal democracies in the West including majority democracies (Britain), consensus democracies (United States) and parliamentary democracies (France and Italy) have some form of consistent functional "loyal" opposition, which tries to shape national debates and public policies through partisan or non-partisan political activities and coalitions. What is the situation in Africa?

Since the early 1990s, multipartyism has once again become one of the most important instruments of political reform in Africa. Multipartyism is popularly perceived as the most legitimate channel to transfer or share power and to participate in the political process, especially by the middle class, the working class, and university students. Opposition political parties have mushroomed all over Africa, especially in urban areas. The quest for a basis for new development or social progress is also being carried out, primarily by coalitions or alliances of various class interests, ideologies, and popular movements.

This chapter critically examines the discourses of selected African opposition parties, identifies their objectives and their ideological foundations, and projects the role they play in the current de-construction and reconstruction of African Society. It analyzes opposition party theories as they emerge from within African conditions and examines the kind of societies they propose. The inquiry is a search for a theory of political opposition.

Although different illustrations are derived from many parts of the continent, allowing a comprehensive view of opposition parties in Africa, this book pays particular attention to Côte d'Ivoire and the Democratic Republic of Congo (former Zaïre) because: (1) after the death of Félix Houphouët-Boigny on December 7, 1993, the transition has been relatively and unexpectedly smoother than that of many other countries (with respect to the existing constitution); and (2) in Zaïre, Mobutu, by resisting real political reforms for the past seven years (1990 to 1997), paralyzed the country and destroyed the social base for nation-building; and (3) the arrival of the Alliance of Democratic Forces for the Liberation of Congo (ADFLC) on the national political scene as a populist revolutionary movement has also made this case interesting. Clearly, it has changed the equation of power between the opposition parties in the country. On May 15, 1997, Mobutu fled the country. On May 23, 1997, Laurent-Désiré Kabila, formed a transitional union government with 13 ministers of whom 7 represent the alliance and, as expected, with no representation from the Mobutuist allies. Other ministers were nominated later. The Democratic Republic of Congo, with its regional and national strengths, has inspired many opposition parties in countries such as Cameroon, Kenya, and the Sudan; however, it has also threatened the ruling parties in most countries in Africa.

Since October 1996, the war that started in the eastern region of Zaïre, which was started by the Banyamulenge (the Tutsis from South Kivu), and the Banyamasisi (the Tutsis from North Kivu), and led by Laurent-Désiré Kabila, the leader of the ADFLC, the Mobutuist regime was seriously challenged on every ground as it had been in 1964 by the Mulelist movement (the Simba and the Mai-Mai) and by the Shaba 1 and 2 in 1978 and 1979 (the invasions of the Shaba's province by the ex Katangese secessionists and other Congolese antiMobutuists), respectively. In capturing territory and power in most parts of the country and finally taking over state power in Kinshasa on May 17, 1997 with armed struggle in a form of popular revolutionary approach, Laurent-Désiré Kabila has also challenged the current discourses of the opposition parties in the Democratic Republic of Congo. In the past seven years or so, the opposition has been deeply divided, but at the same time, it has also been radicalized by the people. The Banyamulenge movement, as a significant force within the ADFLC, made an important contribution to the process of uniting (though temporarily) most of the opposition parties as they saw the Mobutuist regime internally weakened. Finally, Mobutu was disgracefully forced out to exile and died in Morocco on September 7, 1997 with prostate cancer. The study of the opposition in the struggle for power in the Democratic Republic of Congo, focusing on Mobutu's era, is likely to reflect the future political configurations of the country in the 21st century and beyond.

Some questions guiding this analysis include: What is the ideological foundation of the opposition parties within existing multiparty politics in Africa? What are the policy implications of this foundation? A comparative-historical analysis of what the opposition parties say and do, and how they conduct themselves in political arenas, will help identify what they have in common in terms of behavioral trends and ideological bases. This is important for further identifying the characteristics of African democracy and the kind of society the African parties' leaders would like to create. In the multiparty democratic systems adopted in Africa, the role of opposition parties has apparently become vital or central to political discourse. In the media, parties, clubs, fields, and on the streets in Africa, the degree of democracy in most countries can be measured (symbolically or substantially) by the nature and the degree of activism of opposition parties, by the political space given to them by the ruling party, the government, or captured by members of opposition themselves.

A GENERAL HISTORICAL PERSPECTIVE

After the failure of the nationalistic and militaristic policies of the African petty bourgeoisie and the African Marxist regimes of the 1960s and 1970s to formulate and implement relevant policies that could positively transform living conditions and the political economies of most people, the majority of Africans, especially farmers, peasants, working classes, women, and the lumpen-proletarians, are once again attempting to rise up to re-organize themselves in an extremely difficult global and national socioeconomic and political environment. For many, multiparty democracy is associated with a search for the mechanisms to improve their social and economic conditions, despite skepticism based on past experiences.

In spite of problematic issues raised by scholars concerning the assumption of linking development to democracy[1] and the lack of substantial empirical evidence to support such an assumption in Africa, most students of politics agree that there cannot be any broad social progress or social transformation in any society until its people fully and consciously participate or become actively involved in societal projects; that is to say, until the people of that country become consciously engaged in building ideologies and institutions. As indicated in the previous chapter, recently, in Africa, many people have come to believe that, given the global change that is taking place in the world, their demands for participation should be viewed as an important step toward the realization of democratic rights. These rights should be defined as a means of accelerating economic and social development. As mentioned in the first chapter, the opposition parties have preached the antinomy vis-à-vis the state that characterized the level of the general distrust between the state and society, especially the civil society.[2]

Although it is obvious that opposition parties in Africa want to capture state power, it is simplistic to conclude with certainty that capturing power is philosophically an end in itself. To understand where some of them are coming from, other questions must be asked like: Why do they want to take power in an era in which most African economies have been almost completely unproductive have sustained little growth, and have been marginalized from the world system? What would they do with the power or the conditions they inherit? Do the opposition parties come with social and ideological projects? It is difficult to generalize and quantify the objectives and agendas of opposing political parties in Africa; however, general trends can be identified.

The history of their formation, the political culture (beliefs, ideologies, and attitudes) of societies, and the role of the country and state in the international political economy are neither similar nor identical. International division of labor and globalization of capital and productive forces are attempts to homogenize the demands and behavior made on the opposition parties. However, the parties' objectives and behavior depend a great deal on factors such as their origins, the nature and history of social classes, the socioeconomic and political conditions in the milieux in which they have emerged and operated, the influence and legacy of the colonial and neo-colonial powers, and the level of their communication technologies.

Different political parties have had different *raisons d'être* and different agendas. For instance, the African National Congress (ANC), the ruling party in South Africa, and the South West African People's Organization (SWAPO) in Namibia have differed from the Democratic Party of Mwai Kibaki in Kenya, the *Mouvement Populaire de la Révolution* (MPR) of Mobutu in Zaïre, the *Parti Démocratique de la Côte d'Ivoire* (PDCI), the Islamic Salvation Front (FIS) in Algeria, and the National Democratic Alliance in the Sudan (NDA), in terms of their political culture, their strategies to acquire power, their objectives, and their targets. In the Sudan, the main objective of the NDA has been to overthrow the Islamic fundamentalist military regime of El Bashir in Khartoum.[3] The adoption of Islam as a state religion, its underlying political philosophy, and the civil war are the major issues here. In South Africa, for more than three centuries the struggle was based on the right of the African people (especially blacks) to live as citizens and the opportunity to politically exercise that right. In a country like Côte d'Ivoire, the struggle has been based on how to maintain and share power or participate in the political process, and the claim to equal distribution of revenues. In Southern Africa, the element of race has always been one of the most important factors in both the political and ideological formations of the state, and public policy formation and implementation. In countries like Côte d'Ivoire, Burkina Faso, Ghana, Kenya, Liberia, Mali, Morocco, Togo, and Congo-Zaïre, the class origin of the ruling power and its relations to the international capitalist economy has played a more determining role in the policy process of the allocation and distribution of resources.

Mobilized for non-ethnic objectives (political parties) as well, the complicated ethnic factor is also an important force in the way liberal democracy is practically conceived, organized, and promoted in Africa. In addition, the cultural inheritance of colonial administration makes a difference in the way people have been socialized. The elements of African culture are still strongly present in the way people choose their party affiliations as in well as the way they behave with their leaders. However, from the institutional and behavioral points of view, theoretically, some generalizations can be made concerning the parties' objectives.

THEORIZING ABOUT OPPOSITION POLITICAL PARTIES IN AFRICA

First, in the writings of theorists like Ibn Khaldun, Plato, Aristotle, Karl Marx, Machiavelli, Max Weber, Amilcar Cabral, Kwame Nkrumah, Nelson Mandela, Oginga Odinga, and Julius Nyerere, regardless of their ideological, intellectual, and philosophical differences, there is a consensus that societal change cannot occur as a natural phenomenon. Political community can change either by class struggles, power struggles, elections, or revolts. Political power changes if state power is either penetrated with concrete purposes of making reforms (new inputs) or taken over by people with revolutionary or nationalistic agendas. State power does not change by its own will. Aristotle talks about the immortality of the *polis* ("city-state"). Kwame Nkrumah believed that the search for "political immortality was the solution for eternal life." He also advocated class struggle as a means of radically transforming power systems. By this logic, the opposition parties, as legally and legitimate political formations in a given social context, should be concerned about either how to obtain state power, or how to influence it.

Second, institutional opposition movements since the 1980s in Africa were born out of worsening social and economic conditions at the national level, the crisis of peripheral capitalism at the global level, the collapse of Marxist African regimes, and the power consolidation by the personalized and centralized states. All these factors had a direct impact on the nature of the *conjoncture Africaine* (used in this context to characterize the African economic malaise), which provoked social dissatisfactions and anger. Third, in many cases, the opposition movements started with the intelligentsia at universities (mostly state-owned schools), in the existing ruling parties, within the trade unions, and outside the continent among exiled Africans (intellectuals and former members of the ruling parties).

In theorizing about the ideological tendencies of the opposition parties, their social base and their intended objectives, this book discusses the deontology of being in the opposition in Africa. As already indicated, this is not a case-by-case analysis. The generalization concerns what it means to be in opposition parties struggling against the dominant or ruling party. One of the working assumptions is that a state with a long history of political struggle (both inside and outside the country) against the ruling party or the state, before the emergence of multipartyism, is more likely to produce opposition parties with clear agendas than a state with a short history of political struggle. An opposition party with a clear ideology and political agenda creates a solid ground for political debates.

The question of what opposition parties want, in Kenya for example, was clearly articulated by the major opposition parties before the Kenya general elections in December 1992. It was clear that Kibaki, Matiba, and the late Odinga wanted to challenge the Kenya African National Union (KANU), the ruling party since the country earned its independence from the British. Jomo Kenyatta had been its leader in the early 1960s. It was not clear, however, how to make this challenge effective (what strategies to use). Kibaki and the late Odinga had been vice presidents of KANU at different times; therefore, they were insiders. Most of the opposition parties had one thing in common: they were all against totalitarianism and the power monopoly of KANU and its leader Daniel arap Moi. Each leader of the opposition party, especially within the Forum for Democracy (FORD), wanted to become party president. Each wanted to present his own candidacy for the presidential elections. The bigger picture was how to capture state power and defeat Moi and his party in both presidential and legislative elections. Based on the level of enthusiasm in various constituencies, the leaders of the opposition believed that all social and political conditions were met for this challenge, despite massive resistance and excessive use of force from the ruling party and state to forestall multipartyism. The leaders of the FORD did not split because of some ideological differences. As Michael Chege rightly stated:

The opposition's road on this destiny of grief began with the bickering within the unified FORD about the primary elections to determine the party leadership. It was not essentially a battle of "tribes" for power as Kenya's ruling party and most of the media have portrayed it. If Kenyan ethnic groups detested each other so much, there would not have been a FORD in the first place. The party had genuine trans-ethnic representation and its rank and file remained united in their hostility to KANU. On the issue of leadership however, their leaders would not agree. Odinga wanted indirect primary elections in contrast to Motiba and Martin Shikuku who preferred to let the people decide in nation-wide primaries. And as if one major split in the opposition was not enough, Mwal Kibaki jumped ship from KANU in December 1991 and founded the Democratic Party.[4]

Although the opposition in Kenya had a long history of struggle against Moi, especially Mwa Kenya, an underground movement, the opposition leaders used poor judgment when they have believed that, despite internal divisions and struggles for power, they could still defeat Moi. As reflected in the 1992 elections, the competitive politics in Kenya were very much personalized and disorganized, leaving the interests of people aside. The traditions of the loyal opposition were not combined with new strategies related to the dynamic of the milieu. The parliament, and technically the court, have been the only political spaces for the opposition parties to defeat Moi or challenge the proposed policies of the KANU. Despite the unpopularity of Daniel arap Moi among most Kenyans, the political opposition in Kenya lost the December 1997 presidential election to Moi, once again. Many people in Kenya believe that the elections were probably rigged because the ruling Kenya African National Union, not only controls resources, but it also has power to allocate them to whoever can support its platform. However, it should also be noted that despite the complexity of the political situation in Kenya, the 13 challengers (presidential candidates) did not agree on creating well-thought collective sets of political strategies to be used against Moi. The nearest challengers—Mwai Kibaki, Raili Odinga, and Michael Wamalwa did not articulate their candidacies through the framework of an opposition coalition with a common objective to challenge Moi. Rather, each of them was running to secure the largest piece of the pie; that is to say, to be the next president of Kenya.

As articulated earlier in this chapter, the behavior of the opposition politics in Kenya can be generalized to African politics at large. Why cannot this opposition agree on what is to be done? Why do members of the opposition parties in most countries in Africa wait until the results of the elections are announced to declare that they do not accept them? Are the opposition politics in Africa affected by inertia or are they philosophically opportunistic? Do they have an amnesia about the intrigues of the ruling party?

What have been the dominant strategies of the opposition political parties in Congo-Zaïre? Since Mobutu came to power on November 24, 1965 through a military coup d'état, he has been confronted with three major opposition movements, which can ideologically be grouped into

1. The Lumumbaists, or those associated with the ideology of the progressive government

of Stanleyville in the 1960s, both before and after the assassination of Prime Minister Patrice Lumumba in January 1961.
2. The secessionists, or those associated with the ideology of separatism.
3. The accommodationists, or those who fought to either integrate Mobutuism or replace it with a similar political agenda.

This categorization is far from perfect. However, for the sake of clarity, it represents current major ideological tendencies needed for understanding the origins of Zaïrean opposition parties and their underlying philosophical bases.

Lumumbaists attempted, based on either idealism or opportunism, to raise issues concerning nation-building in Congo-Zaïre. They believed that an ideology of unity or a radical progressive nationalism could advance social progress in the country with respect to the goals of Patrice Lumumba. How could this happen? In the early 1960s, Lumumbaists succeeded in attaining two important goals: the consolidation of a strong ideological alliance with the then Eastern European bloc during the Cold War, and the organization and promotion of a second independence movement (Nzongola-Ntalaja, 1987, 92). Starting from Kwilu, and rapidly reaching over almost all the Congo with Lumumbaism as its ideological base, the struggle, starting in 1964 as a second independence movement, was crushed by 1967 by the intervention of the West, notably France, the United States, Belgium, and a few African countries. This military crush, however, did not succeed in dismantling Lumumbaism as an ideology. Even Mobutu used it to enhance his own power, popularize his policies, expand his political base, and consolidate his power. Although there has not been a single political agenda among all Lumumbaists on how to promote the ideology of a united country and nation, democracy, and social justice, many believed that the change in the Democratic Republic of Congo should occur at the level of both ideology and personality politics. Mobutu and Mobutuism must leave state power. That is not to say that all those who called themselves Lumumbaists have absolutely been against Mobutu. In fact, many have worked with him and continue to work for him in different capacities; however, the dominant political position among Lumumbaists has always been that Mobutu is ruining the country and should not continue to rule, for ideological and social reasons. From this point of view, theoretically, the opposition parties have been advocating structural change.

The secessionists believe in the political independence of each major sub-region of the Democratic Republic of Congo. Especially in the case of the Katangan secessionist movement, this ideology had its roots in colonial policies.[5] It is not necessarily the internal weaknesses or deficiencies of African culture and ethnicity that forced Tshombe and Munongo to secede. Secessionism was a political instrument used by the Katangan and South Kasaian elite (notably Albert Kalonji) to promote particular class interests. Despite the authoritarian and totalitarian systems imposed on the country by Joseph-Désiré Mobutu since November 25, 1965, the strength of this ideology (secessionism) was not eliminated. Secessionism can succeed because, from the point of view of some natives, its dynamism is still based on emotional and cultural arguments and beliefs. Mobutu's policies of favoritism and his quota, for instance, in the education system, further contributed to secessionism. He reinforced this trend by developing clientist politics. Using the well-known premise of *diviser pour reigner* ("divide to rule"), he disoriented his clients by giving them an impression of sharing wealth but not power through co-option, random promotion, and political appointments and dismissals. The client-petty bourgeoisie did not have a strong class base. That is to say, the clientist bourgeoisie had neither power nor wealth. From a class perspective there are always dynamic relations between power and wealth, in a capitalist sense. One can produce the other and vice-versa. To better understand the above ideological categorizations and the nature of the opposition's discourses, a brief discussion on how the opposition parties emerged is essential.

With strong internal social pressures caused by deteriorating economic conditions, the weakening of highly centralized state bureaucracies, and political turmoil in the former Eastern bloc, Mobutu reluctantly announced, on April 24, 1990, the birth of multipartyism to avoid massive uprisings and a violent end to his regime. He then proposed establishing a limited (guided) democratic system with two other parties. The *Union pour la Démocratie et le Progrès Social* (UDPS), led by Etienne Tshisekedi wa Mulumba, co-founder of the MPR and a former minister of interior and minister of justice in Mobutu's regime, was among the first parties that accepted this option. Although Tshisekedi had seriously opposed Mobutu for more than a decade, at the beginning, his party did not clearly articulate a viable nationalist ideology and agenda with a vision of a new society. That is to say, there was a lack of a clear political project. UDPS could therefore be characterized as a product of the power struggle rather than the ideological struggle. In addition, UDPS had previously experienced a division between radicals and moderates. Until recently, its constituency was dominated by an ethnic alliance (Luba), though this did not diminish Tshisekedi's political ambition and populism. Because of centralization of power in the party, as well as strategies the party had used in the past, Tshisekedi gave the impression that he was interested more in power than democracy. After Kabila's announcement of the new government on May 22, 1997, the UDPS declared itself to be in opposition to the newly established ruling party as because Tshisekedi is not part of this new transitional government. Tshisekedi refused to recognize the new government.

The *Parti Démocratique et Social Chrétien* (PDSC), whose members were dominated by Christians and Kimbanguists (members of the African Independent Church), is led by Ileo-Nzango Amba, a former *bras droit* of Mobutu for many years and president of the National Assembly under Mobutu's regime. Amba shares ethnic affinity with Mobutu. Ideologically, his party is not dissociated from Mobutuism, though its program of action is based on peace, justice, and charity. Inspired and supported by the European Christian Democratic parties, PDSC has not been able to mobilize the non-Christian masses in rural areas. Parties such as the *Front Commun des Nationalistes* (FCN) of Bula Nyati or Kamanda, whose leaders were active members of the MPR and often cabinet ministers of Mobutu, had tendencies of political opportunism. Kamanda wa Kamanda is the last Mobutu's minister of foreign affairs. In August 1997, he made a call from Brussels, Belgium to Congolese to join him in an opposition to Kabila's government. The main objective of the new movement of *Rassemblement des Patriotes Congolais* (RPC) is to overthrow the Kabila's government, which he characterized to be a regime of occupation and undemocratic.

Only a few parties, like the *Mouvement National Congolais/Lumumba* (MNC/L), led by François-Patrice Tolenga Lumumba, the socialist party, and the *Parti des Lumumbistes Unifiés* (Palu) of Antoine Gizenga, apparently did not have ideological ties to the MPR. The *Rassemblement Démocratique de la République* (RDR) of Mungul Diaka articulated anti-Mobutu slogans. However, it should be noted that Mungul Diaka had worked not through a coalition government, but for Mobutu in several ministerial capacities in the past. Highly elitist, the FCN did not have any strong roots in the social, economic, and political conditions of the poor, who comprise the majority of the people. The FCN, for instance, is composed of intellectuals who do not seem to be comfortable with the MPR. Their aspiration is to acquire power.

As social protests intensified, the regime was threatened with losing its support, even among the coalition of various members of the old political school. Thus, Mobutu attempted to impose a new constitution on the people. Between April and July 1990, there were more than 70 political formations in the country. In March 1991, 19 legally recognized parties prepared to contest the legislative and presidential elections originally planned for April 1991. Twenty-three opposition parties grouped in the *Front Uni* were interested more in setting up a democratic process than in replacing Mobutu per se. In April 1991, Mobutu accepted the idea of a national conference with a clear agenda of hijacking it, but the opposition parties insisted that Mobutu should resign before the conference. In June 1991, more than 100 parties, many of which did not fulfill Mobutu's requirements, were organized. Mobutu attempted to sabotage the process by offering cabinet posts and other ministerial positions to members of the opposition parties. As indicated in the previous chapters, the conflict between the popular movements' objectives and those of the political parties' essentially elitist groupings slowed down the process of democratic struggle. Democracy, as perceived in this context, has mainly become a process of elite political maneuvering to acquire power.

Until recently there were three dominant positions within the democratic opposition in Zaïre. There were those who tended to think that it was impossible to achieve democratic objectives in popular movements without forming coalitions with Mobutu. These groups called accommodationists tended to see themselves as realists. They worked to share power with the regime and opportunistically accepted the regime's cosmetic proposals. Nguza Karl-I-Bond was essentially the most opportunistic of all, based on his acrobatic political history. For support, he counted mostly on his ethnic affiliations in Shaba Province. He was always close to Mobutu and accepted permanent positions in Mobutu's government. Then there were those who believed in embarking on a strategy of advocating and using political violence. For them, the language that Mobutu understood best was militarism, regardless of cost. Although Laurent-Désiré Kabila operated outside of the rules of civil society, there are some opposition parties in Kinshasa who supported his approach. There is also still a small group of idealists who see popular movements as opportunities to debate on the nature of the society that the majority of the people in the Democratic Republic of Congo would like to create. It is believed that the idealist discourses should engender new ideas about where the society should go.

Among the relatively recent political formations in Congo-Zaïre, more than 200 since September 1993, many have as their basis: class, ethnicity, regionalism, and religion. They clearly articulated the position that Mobutu should leave his position and let people put their homes in order according to their tastes and their local, social, and political realities. This position is based on the idea that no one from outside a locality or region can understand and appreciate the local needs as well as the local people. Mobutu's past public policies reinforced this kind of position. Whether one agrees with this logic or not, further deterioration of social and economic conditions in most regions provides the basis and justification for secessionist discourses within existing political parties. No region in Zaïre has been economically better off, including Mobutu's own home region, with perhaps the exception of his constructed village (Gbadolite) or *fief à la* Yamoussoukro (the late Félix Houphouët-Boigny's village in Côte d'Ivoire). Economically, the region of Bandaka, *Equateur* is no better off as far as social progress is concerned than any other regions or sub-regions such as Kivu, Kasai, or Kwilu. The secessionist tendency seems to appeal to many people as a natural political choice for those who do not have any other means to survive. For them, democracy has to promote a highly decentralized society and power structure, with each region having complete autonomy. Some people in this categorization envision Zaïre either as a federation similar to the new Ethiopian model (a federation model based on ethnicity) or as a confederation of loose political regions. Ethnicity is an important element upon which discourses within this ideological tendency are articulated.

Accommodationist tendencies in the opposition parties implied the acceptance and incorporation of Mobutuism into the general political discourse in Zaïre. One may define this as a class ideological choice, or as already indicated, clientism. This tendency transcends ethnicity or regionalism. It is primarily based on opportunism. Most of its advocates are intellectuals—professors or university graduates.

The *Union Sacrée* (US) was still the biggest political forum in Zaïre when ADFLC took over the country. It was composed of several major parties, each with its own ideological orientation. Its main objective was to explore strategies to get rid of Mobutu legally. This coalition was not ideologically based; rather, it was a strategic instrument used by the opposition parties to fight Mobutu. It called for a national conference and the establishment of a transitional government. To the US, getting rid of Mobutu was a prerequisite for the democratic struggle. Does this guarantee the establishment of democracy? Is the idea of a government of national unity necessarily democratic? In reality, a government of national unity may not be democratic if the process for its establishment is undemocratic.

Historically the question of what the opposition wants is still relevant even after the new regime has been established in the Democratic Republic of Congo. To attempt to answer this question, one must identify the leaders of the opposition and social class to which they belong. It is difficult to provide quantitative answers because democracy is an ongoing process in Africa.

Tshisekedi, Kengo, Mungul Diaka, Ileo, Nendaka, Nguza Karl-i-Bond, Kamitatu, Kamanda wa Kamanda, and Kazadi (all of whom are members of the old Binza's bourgeoisie or their young associates) want some political change in Congo-Zaïre. But what kind of change do they pursue? First, many of these opposition leaders wanted to replace Mobutu. For many of them, as Tshisekedi said in August 1991 when he was nominated prime minister and refused to take the oath in front of him, Mobutu was a monster. Second, their concept of struggle has been more of a power struggle until recently, rather than that of a class or an ideological struggle. What does this mean? It means that their target was Mobutu. In a typical strategy of power struggle, they concentrated on the personal weaknesses of the target.

Unlike the opposition parties in Côte d'Ivoire, where the university community was mobilized as the center for political formations, in Zaïre the universities have often been decentralized, demobilized, and closed since the beginning of multipartyism. Consequently, they collectively played an insignificant role in the formation of larger political parties. Private universities seem to have little interest in national politics. Sub-regional development was their main concern. There were parties of intelligentsia like the one of Kamanda wa Kamanda, but they did not have their base at the universities. For example, political discourses in Zaïre have not always resembled to those associated with Professor Wodié's political discourses, for example, which are basically intellectualistic, highly philosophical, and abstract.[6] However, it should be noted that the power struggles of the opposition parties in Zaïre have gradually been changing into an ideological struggles because of popular pressure, which has accelerated because of the arrogance of Mobutu and his ruling party, the MPR. The opposition parties in Zaïre have not been as static as many people seemed to have believed earlier. However, the social and economic conditions in which they have been operating are extremely difficult. They have radicalized themselves by popular actions. The resistance of the ruling party and state to any serious democratic discourse was an important factor that contributed to the consciousness raising of the opposition and the people at large.

In other countries, such as Côte d'Ivoire, radicalism has been part of some parties' ideological choices from the beginning. There are no social indicators that show that even after the death of President Félix Houphouët-Boigny, parties are likely to radicalize themselves as they did in Zaïre and consequently radicalize the masses because of the inflexibility or arrogance of the *Parti Démocratique Ivoirien-Rassemblement Démocratique Africain* (PDI-RDA). Moreover, the actions of the *Front Populaire Ivoirien* (FPI), a popular party, do not appear to be further radicalizing the people. On the contrary, the actions of the FPI seem to alienate many. Until recently, there have been about eight functioning leftist parties in Côte d'Ivoire whose leaders opted for radical leftist ideologies from the time they were formed to guide their discourses and actions. Although they did not proclaim to be Marxist or socialist, as will be discussed later, they combined some elements of leftist nationalism, and populism.

In Nigeria, the military regime thought that it was possible to militarily control the behavior of the two imposed opposition parties and the outcome of their performance by nominating pro-Babangida people for various posts in the constitutional commission and the government, thereby polarizing the parties. Babangida's behavior contributed to the radicalization of the Social Democratic Party (SDP), whose candidate seemingly won the presidential elections of June 1993. Babangida's government canceled the results. The leaders of both political parties were close to the military regime. Since December 1993, General Abacha, the current Nigerian head of state, has organized debates on the constitution, an activity which has become expected and routine in many African countries, especially in military regimes. A new constitution was produced in 1996. Many Nigerians saw this call for constitutional debate as another maneuver set up by Abacha and his clique to remain in power for many years beyond 1998. Is this a phenomenon of déjà vu? Babangida's behavior kept many Nigerians from forming political opposition parties, though he did not destroy their basis. True opposition to the military regime in Nigeria has come from various professional organizations and people, although the SDP under Moshood Abiola continues to mobilize voices. However, these organizations also have strong regionalist sentiments. These sentiments tend to weaken the strength of the organizations in terms of the sense of common objectives to be pursued. If General Abacha and his clique do not exit from state power soon, Nigeria is likely to get further into fire and disturbances, unless the regime transforms itself into a semi-civilian government with a guided democracy, based on a clear process of recruitment for public office, without going through any electoral rituals.

Besides the US in Congo-Zaïre, which is purely a strategically functioning rather than an ideological, political coalition, there are minority leftist groups and *partis alimentaires* ("sponsored parties"). Many of these *parti alimentaires* were formed with strong and special relations with the ruling party, the MPR of Mobutu. Ideologically, they were not qualitatively different from Mobutuism, though they also talked about democratic struggle as a means to save the country from its current social, economic, and political *marasme* ("wasting away"). They tended to be more antagonistic to Lumumbaism than secessionism. Their discourses were power centered, rather than democracy centered. Given the level of resistance to change from Mobutu and his party and the harsh social, conditions in the country, the only remaining option, as articulated in April 1994 by some members of the US in Zaïre, was the use of armed struggle to overthrow Mobutu and establish some form of democracy. Mobutu himself was not neutral as far as the massacre of Kasai people in the Shaba and Kivu provinces between 1992 and 1994 goes. The conflicts orchestrated and organized by Mobutu continued to discredit the opposition's work. The nature of democratic discourses in the Democratic Republic of Congo and in Côte d'Ivoire, can be systematically compared in general terms.

As indicated earlier, Côte d'Ivoire and the Democratic Republic of Congo, as independent and contemporary states, came to the scene of international power struggles through different strategies. They chose different paths of organizing, advancing, and maintaining state interests. That is to say, the histories of political formations and state-building in these two countries qualitatively differ.

What have the ideological and intellectual orientations in the discourses and actions of the opposition in Côte d'Ivoire been? In comparison to political situations in many other countries in sub-Saharan Africa, Côte d'Ivoire under the late Félix Houphouët-Boigny enjoyed considerable political stability, in relative terms, for many years. In Côte d'Ivoire, one might even have gotten the impression that there was a consensus of ideologies and values. With a stable state (patrician and elite), a growing middle class, flourishing cocoa and coffee production and marketing, reflected by the increase in the gross national product (GNP) and the dominance of foreign investments, especially those of France, in the 1970s Côte d'Ivoire was considered by many as being ready to take off. Why is it that Rostow's theory did not succeed here as the Ivorian people, especially the middle class, had expected? W. Rostow, a well-known American economist has produced paradigms to economic development that should take place through fixed stages. Modernization scholars generalized those stages to study the social, political, and economic conditions in developing countries. What went wrong in Ivorian policy formation and implementation? A brief analysis of the history of political conditions is needed to explain understand how the state related to society and how opposition parties later emerged.

Samir Amin has indicated that the big challenge for Côte d'Ivoire then was for the state to mobilize resources for the use of the agricultural sector to support manufacturing and industrialization projects (1967). In other words, the challenge was how to transform the agricultural sector through capital and intensive labor into an industrial process, and how to create a strong local capital and investment base. If this challenge could have been taken seriously and addressed effectively, probably Côte d'Ivoire would have transcended the characteristics of the peripheral capitalist economy and joined the orbit of capitalism with its internal dynamics and contradictions, as did the newly industrialized countries in Asia. However, without a consistent policy of large-scale agricultural production (massive mechanization that would lead to the transformation of productive forces), Côte d'Ivoire could not take off without creating a national industrial base. In some sectors of the Ivorian public sector, there have been efforts to modernize without industrializing.

From the mid-1970s, Ivorians talked about *la conjoncture* or *la fin du miracle mirage* ("illusionary miracle") as part of daily conversations that reflected high living standards in the country and high national indebtedness. But unlike the Democratic Republic of Congo or Ghana after Kwame Nkrumah, Côte d'Ivoire had a single political party that succeeded in managing the affairs of state for many years, so it maintained a stable state, a bureaucracy bound by regulations, and a relatively conservative prosperous middle class. As a main goal, this state gave itself the creation of the Ivorian nation. The *Syndicat Agricole Africain* (SAA) was formed in 1944 by seven Ivorian plantation owners. At the time of its formation, the main objective of its members was not necessarily to challenge existing colonial power structures or to struggle for power sharing. Their interest was mainly economic; SAA members wanted to sell their cocoa and other agricultural products at the same price granted to French farmers.[7]

Gradually, as the contradictions of the colonial economy and those of state intensified, this economic grouping, having attracted unexpected popular support, was transformed into a political organization in 1946: the RDA with its branch, the PDCI. Félix Houphouët-Boigny, cofounder of the SAA and first chairman of the RDA, was the president of Côte d'Ivoire from 1960, when the country was granted nominal political independence by France, until his death in December 1993.

Until recently, the PDCI-RDA, the state-party for more than three decades, was a hierarchical, elitist party, with a strong social base in rural areas. It took advantage of its historical origins (*parti des paysans-planteurs*) ("party of peasant farmers") to claim legitimacy. Despite some internal power struggles within the party in the 1950s and 1960s, the state party ruled the country with apparently traditional consensus *à la Baoulé*, that is to say, in a manner very close to the Baoulé system of governance. There were no major political and legal challenges until April 30, 1990, when the late President Houphouët-Boigny announced the legalization of opposition parties and the intent to hold multiparty elections.

By the end of the 1980s, *la conjoncture* was intensified by the collapse of the international market for cocoa, one of the major export products in Côte d'Ivoire. This economic crisis greatly contributed to the events that led to the emergence of multipartyism. The PDCI-RDA was, as were other ruling parties in Africa, reluctant to accept the establishment of multipartyism. Finally, to respond to tremendous national and international pressures and avoid a generalized social crisis that could lead to a massive political crisis, Henri Konan Bédié, now the president of Côte d'Ivoire, who was then president of the National Assembly, announced the birth of multipartyism.

Before April 1990 the FPI, the first major leftist political organization, was led by the party's general secretary (and president) Laurent Gbagbo, who had been in prison between February and July 1992. He acted almost alone as the organizer of a populist power struggle movement challenging the ruling party without having a strong national social and political base. The movement was popularized and publicized in the 1970s by the international media, especially those from France where Gbagbo went into exile. While in France, he developed an alliance with the French socialists. In Côte d'Ivoire many people called him such names as "betrayer," "power hungry," and "adventurer." The French Socialist Party supported the FPI, at least at the beginning. The actions of the FPI at the time were based on massive criticism of the "immortality" claimed by President Félix Houphouët-Boigny. The power struggle approach could not bear positive fruits unless a national democratic struggle was organized, because the leader of the FPI was an outsider to the political machinery of the Ivorian state. About 40 parties were formed after April of 1990, of which only 20 somehow functioned until the 1995 elections. The most important of the parties with leftist ideological tendencies include the *Parti Ivoirien du Travail* (PIT), the *Union Sociale Démocratique* (USD), the *Parti Socialiste Ivoirien* (PSI), and the *Mouvement Démocratique et Social* (MDC).

What is the social basis of some of these parties and what do they wish to accomplish? Identification of some of their major behavioral and ideological tendencies provides us a comprehensive picture of the oppositions' discourse in Côte d'Ivoire. It should be stressed that unlike in Zaïre, where the major opposition parties emerged from within the ruling party of MPR of Mobutu of (the MPR), in Côte d'Ivoire the major opposition parties came from outside of the state apparatus and the PDCI-RDA. They originated as university-based organizations with teachers and students as the major actors. Most party leaders were strongly associated with the SYNARES, which is the *syndicat* ("union") of higher education teachers. Parties were formed to make *revendications* ("demands") especially for the rights of citizens. Until recently, the FPI has been organizationally broader and more sophisticated in political recruitment than other advanced opposition parties. The FPI held its Constitutive Congress between February 19 and 20, 1988.[8]

The FPI's activism influenced many other social and political groups and individuals. It is the only party that fulfilled all requirements for presenting a candidacy in the November 1990 presidential election. Laurent Gbagbo was the only leader of the opposition parties who dared to openly challenge the regime of Félix Houphouët-Boigny.

From its activism as a populist movement to its transformation into legal political party, the FPI has been consistent in articulating its objectives. Moïse Koumoué in the FPI's statement of March 3, 1990 and in other occasions, has repeatedly stated (prior to the event of February 18, 1992, in which the party was accused of acts of vandalism and breaking the law), that the FPI was ready to take over state power to govern and to apply its own social, economic, and cultural programs.[9]

The FPI was prepared to govern and change economic relations, especially by increasing the price of cocoa for the small producers and small householders. Its activities and its meetings were focused on how to capture state power by all means necessary. However, this objective, which is a normal political objective for any party, dominated the party agenda. However, it also contributed to the isolation of the party from other leftist parties. The FPI refused to accept the concept of the national conference, considering it to be a phenomenon that had been *dépassé* ("superseded"). Although democracy does not necessary mean capturing state power for the FPI, it is believed that this process may give the party an opportunity to penetrate the government and change policies from within the system. Thus, this party has refused to behave and act as a political pressure group *à l'Américaine.* Whether or not its means to reach its objectives are legal and morally acceptable by the people and the government is another story. It is a power-centered party based on ethnicity, although there are members from ethnic groups other than the Bétés. At the beginning of the movement, ethnicity was used as the easiest way to manipulate and mobilize people based on their geographical and linguistic affiliations—emotional and cultural factors that do not require social and national consciousness to be influential.

In Côte d'Ivoire, one of the major issues of discussion before the death of Félix Houphouët-Boigny was the nature of the violence associated with the actions of some political formations, especially the FPI. Many Ivorians tend to perceive the Bétés who dominate the FPI as essentially physical or violent in their behavior.

Thus, they perceive this party as developing and encouraging cultural antagonisms against other ethnic groups, especially the Baoulés. However, sociologically, it is difficult to conclude that the Bétés, or other ethnic groups they associate with, are naturally more violent than any other Ivorian ethnic groups. They have different traditions in the way their society is organized and social relations are carried out. Historically, they have cooperated and worked with other ethnic groups, especially the Baoulé's, concerning the use of the forest for plantations, for instance. Until recently, the "Baoulés" have been welcome in Bété geographical areas. The confrontation that occurred among them in the past originated in a political rather than a cultural struggle, as it has been suggested by most members of the ruling party, PDCI-RDA. Many people in the ruling party perceive the Bétés as culturally violent.

What is the origin of the violence associated with political discourse in the FPI? Four explanations can be articulated. Violence could be

1. A consequence of the frustration of a popular movement that does not seem to have a convincing political agenda.
2. A result of a lack of dialogical relations between the party and other parties, civil society, and the state.
3. A product of the deadlock on the issues of how to share power.
4. An outcome of the misinterpretation of democracy.
5. A product of the culture of the dominant ethnic group within the party. Many people, especially members of the PDCI-RDA, take this explanation more seriously than any other possibility.

Can violence advance democracy in an African context? An appropriate question is, what kind of violence promotes democracy? What are its objectives and who is advancing the violence? Spontaneous violence in itself cannot advance any form of democracy. However, historically, many political struggles in world politics testify that organized political violence with concrete political objectives can succeed in advancing national revolutions in some regions and countries. Amilcar Cabral, Frantz Fanon, Samora Machel, Nelson Mandela, Albert Memmi have rightly indicated in their writings and political actions that the only way to dislodge colonialists is by using a combination of means similar to what the imperialists used. Political violence can be an instrument of either class or power struggle. However, it should not be the basis for the illegal activities of any populist movement. Even Machiavelli's discourse does not see violence as a permanent instrument of power struggle or the maintenance of power. It can be used for specific objectives but cannot become a permanent instrument for advancing the immortality of the state. In short, political violence as an instrument of political discourse should be, in principle, a conscious activity, socially disruptive, but politically constructive. As Henry Bienen believes:

Angola and Mozambique, ex-Portuguese colonies, were held out as examples that would support Frantz Fanon's propositions that individuals and peoples would become whole again and would have a political rebirth by participating in violent politics. . . . Violence was instrumental in creating new societies also because individuals would forge new ties expressed through revolutionary organizations.[10]

Political violence as used in this context is not the equivalent of the indiscriminate outbreaks similar to those that occurred on what is known in Abidjan as "black" Tuesday—February 18, 1992. Society and politics do not change naturally by themselves: their internal contradictions provoke desirable or undesirable changes. How society and politics effectively change, who changes them, and for what objectives depend on social and productive relations, and the political culture of the ruling class. How does one deal with the energies that lead to the material destruction of properties, for example?

First, disruption is a consequence of social and political battles. Second, it is not an end in itself. To deal with it adequately, all social forces in a society and state must enter into serious national dialogue. Although violence should not be supported, the empirical facts show that Bienen, who thinks that violence has not settled issues in Africa beyond the period of anti-colonial struggle, is wrong.[11]

Not all forms of violence are aberrant or pathological in Africa. It depends on the meaning given to the violence and the actors, actresses, or institutions that are involved in violent actions. Recent democratic movements came with a high dose of organized violence. Violence should not necessarily target the elimination of individual members of the dominant class or the whole community on the basis of their ideology (a Stalinist approach), but it should set up a different political means for restructuring society, that is, creating new power relations and mechanisms for distributing power and encouraging participation in politics.

Another leftist political group called the PIT, whose leader is Mr. Francis Wodié, a former representative from Cocody[12] who has also been active in Ivorian politics, should be briefly discussed. In principle, the social base of this party should be the working class. In reality, however, it is a party of intellectuals. Some call it an "intellectualistic party." How can we characterize the PIT?

The PIT has two major characteristics, legalism and an intellectual philosophy. In the reasoning of the PIT leader, decolonization was born out of the contradictions of colonization; therefore, democracy has to engender itself out of the contradictions of non-democratic systems.[13]

A rupture between the search for democracy and the non-democratic culture cannot happen through an evolutionary process or the natural order of things. In the case of Côte d'Ivoire, the contradictions of a one-party state have engendered debates on multiparty politics through the *Conseil National* ("National Council") in which the *journées de dialogue* ("days of dialogue") were state-organized. Multipartyism is an antithesis within Ivorian social formation. That is to say, multipartyism, as a transitional political force, is qualitatively different from one-party state. A one-party state represents discourses associated with thesis. Democracy is considered a synthetical discourse within this logic. The PIT perceives the discourse of multipartyism as a necessity for democracy. Francis Wodié said: "The need for multipartyism stems from a need for a diversity of interests and opinions, which prevails in every free society. Necessarily implemented when tensions are high, multipartyism leads to freedom of choice and the expression of free and equal participation in the political game."[14]

From the above definition, two requisite principles can be derived: liberty and equality, with respect to the diversity of interests, opinions, and choices. These principles cannot be fully expressed by a one-party state because this party is not a product of the social contract. For Wodié, in a transitional Africa, it is only the sovereign national conference that personifies and expresses the will of the state. It was believed that out of the activities of this conference, a new social contract might emerge. This assembly, which should be constituted of national fractions (the people), would become, on the basis of a national consensus, sovereign and representative.[15] As expressed in its ideology, the PIT's discourses do not seem to practically and realistically have any consolidated proletarian base. Wodié has intellectualized and theorized about politics and democracy, but he has not yet given them strong social forms. It is still interesting to look at the PIT's relationship with the trade unions.

Another party that is worth mentioning among leftist political parties is the *Mouvement Démocratique et Social* (MDS). This party also had its base at the National University of Côte d'Ivoire (now Université de Cocody). Its first president was Professor Lanciné Sylla, a specialist in political sociology at the *Institut d'Ethno-Sociologie*. Born in July 1990, MDS, like other leftist parties, was formed by intellectuals. It defined itself as a movement, a laboratory for moving ideas and ideals. It is a movement with the promotion of people's aspirations to social justice, freedom, and respect for fundamental human rights as its major objectives.[16]

The MDS defined itself as a movement of reflection on democracy. In terms of membership or affiliation, it was open to all people regardless of individual religious, ethnic origin or ideological affiliation. It emphasized the agenda of socializing people with democratic ideas and promoting the spirit of democracy with the objective of creating a democratic process and consequently a democratic nation. It prepared to compete in the presidential and legislative elections in 1995. As Kouamé Nguessan, a sociologist who was in charge of the party's external affairs, told me: "Its success will depend on its ability to mobilize members, to advertise its programs, and to finance its actions." The party was considered an educator, and it defined Côte d'Ivoire as being in a non-democratic transition. Its objective was to contribute toward the establishment of the values and norms of a democratic transition.

Between 1990 and early 1994, the political situation in Côte d'Ivoire was characterized by the behavior of a regime in a difficult transition, a *régime de déséquilibre* ("state of disequilibrium") towards democracy. Every transitional situation is fragile, and therefore, unstable. It can shift to either a dictatorship or some form of democracy. Democratization could be pursued in the form of renovations or reforms. For Wodié, this pursuit must be pluralistic and diverse. The sovereign people can opt for any strategy that fits a given social context. Pluralism and diversity must be promoted to create conditions in which democratic discourses can occur.

In short, the transition toward either democracy or dictatorship is a complex phenomenon. For democracy to succeed, there is a need for a high level of tolerance among African people of different political parties, the promotion of respect for differences and laws, and a movement toward the ideal of consensus.

Are parties in such countries as the Cameroon, Côte d'Ivoire, Ghana, Kenya, Nigeria, South Africa, and Congo-Zaïre (under Mobutu) capable of accepting and tolerating differences and promoting the ideal of a nation? The objective of the parties should be first to articulate and advance the culture of democracy and second to actualize this ideal in the policies and processes of production and distribution of resources. The parties must also be self-corrective organizations. President Henri Konan Bédié, when he was president of the National Assembly, perceived this objective in these terms. As he stated during the opening of the parliamentary session:

We have to count on ourselves, on our will to live together in tolerance, with the mutual respect and respect for the laws. The pursuit of a minimum common objective imposes itself on all political parties. Multipartyism is not an end in itself; it has to be a means to expand the well-being to which all citizens sincerely aspire.[17]

What do the opposition parties intend to do to realize their objectives and programs in Burkina Faso? Several factors tend to characterize the current transition toward democracy in Burkina Faso: spirit and the willingness to work hard, and the sense of responsibility and tight military security in Ouagadougou. Here, militarism and nationalism seem to function closely. The important question is what characteristic or tendency will dominate in the process of democratization as the state and society at large are struggling to progress?

The emergence of multiparty democracy in many parts of Africa as indicated earlier was accompanied by strong urban social explosions on the streets. The cases of the Cameroon, Nigeria, and Togo are more telling. Confrontations took the form of physical struggles, massacres, and assassinations. The nature of the explosion varies with social conditions and the political culture of each milieu and its governance. These explosions have exposed and publicized the general state of affairs in Africa and in international political relations. The general process has embodied two major forces through which change was supposed to occur: a national conference and a referendum on the question of a constitution.

In Burkina Faso, the national conference, or national forum, did not complete its course as was the case, for instance, in Bénin, the Congo, Niger, or Togo. This differs from the political process in the Francophone countries in sub-Saharan Africa. Côte d'Ivoire also did not have a national conference. One could easily predict this situation in Côte d'Ivoire, however. In a transitional period without a national conference, politics in Côte d'Ivoire produced an unelected prime minister, Allasane Outtara, and his technocrats. In Burkina Faso, however, it was not possible to predict that their national conference would be sabotaged given its political history of struggle. With the exception of the brutal physical elimination of Sankara and his associates in 1987 and other executions that followed, Burkina Faso did not produce strong social explosions like those in Mali or uprisings that could lead to a coup d'état or social disruption as Congo-Zaïre. Burkina Faso is in a transition, as are other countries that were discussed earlier in this chapter.

Two schools of thought can be considered here. Some Burkinabè believe that the process of democratization as it has taken place in Burkina will lead to the establishment of a political culture needed for fostering a genuine democratic society. As social and economic conditions improve, and with an ethic of hard work, the people's determination, and the introduction of more discipline in the performance of the state apparatus and public administration, people will eventually support the democratic ideal. This ideal has been a reflection of people's social conditions. It is a strong cooperation between the state and the people, which could make democracy a reality. There are those who are skeptical. For them, the behavior of the state is still strongly militaristic, especially when it comes to the question of its security. The state has not separated itself from the traditions of a military regime: tight control and suspicion. It does not seem to have built enough confidence in its actions to allow the political philosophy of multiparty democracy to be reflected in the free flow of ideas (debates) and the free movement of goods and people.

There is a systematic effort by the people and the state, through privatization policies, to improve the living conditions of the majority of people through Structural Adjustment Programs (SAPs). In 1998, Burkina Faso is among the two African countries (Uganda being the other) which should benefit from the newly established debt relief programs of the World Bank. However, the SAPS have not yet qualitatively improved the conditions of the majority of the African people even in so-called success stories.

What do the opposition parties in Burkina Faso wish to promote and establish? How did these opposition parties emerge? From the time multipartyism was legally instituted to the time of presidential and legislative elections, there were a little more than 60 political parties and about 4,000 political associations. However, only 27 political parties participated in the elections. This book will not discuss the political philosophies of all those parties and associations that claimed to be in opposition to the former military regime, which was accused of being dictatorial. Rather, it will focus on the categorization of tendencies.

The democratic process, if simply defined by the preparation of legislative and presidential elections, was said to be quick and efficient in Burkina Faso. It produced its intended objectives in a short period of time: an elected president in December 1991 and elected national assembly members in May 1992. In Burkina Faso, unlike in many other countries in Africa that produced multipartyism, the presidential election took place before the legislative election. The president-elect could influence the course of the legislative elections. Will this process produce the democratic culture that is needed for creating a democratic society? What has been the role of opposition parties and their vision of society, if any? The outcome of this process has been different compared to that in Côte d'Ivoire because of the differences in political culture, social milieux, national political economy, and the nature of the legitimacy of the ruling parties, among other factors. Is it fair to hypothesize that Blaise Compaoré, the president of Burkina, his party, and his regime have only changed their uniforms in order to legitimize themselves? The answer cannot be that simple. It should be said, however, that as of early 1993 about three-fourths of the members of the ministerial cabinet in Compaoré's civilian government were from opposition parties. Seventeen parties out of 27 have seats in the parliament. Three out of the five declared Sankarist parties that participated in the legislative elections did not win any seats in the parliament. Has Sankara been completely rejected in Burkina? What does that mean in an analysis of the nature of democratic processes and discourses in Africa?

Burkina Faso has come to the current dilemma of the democratic process from a background of popularism and the spirit of the Sankarist-Compaorist revolution that begun in 1983. In addition, it has a history of having one of the strongest trade union movements in West Africa. The major political parties in Burkina Faso include the *Union Nationale pour la Défense de la Démocratie* (UNDD), which was inspired by the ideological tendencies of the *Rassemblement Démocratique Africain* (RDA), the grand old party of the first generation of the Francophone West African elite, the *Alliance pour la Démocratie et la Fédération* (ADF); and the *Mouvement des Démocrates et Patriotes* (MDP); and the *Rassemblement Social Démocratique Independant* of the well-known historian Joseph Ki-Zerbo. All seem to agree that the struggle for democracy has to be part of a struggle to improve people's material and social conditions. Despite Burkina Faso's long history of trade unionism, the current major political parties do not seem to emphasize the working-class ideological affinity between the parties.

Many parties joined the government to make internal policy reforms possible. In other parties, the opposition has been silent; they joined the government because of a lack of clear ideological convictions. Non-conventional opposition parties, those that operate outside of the legal national jurisdiction, continue to see this transition in Burkina Faso as undemocratic. Many believe that Compaoré is the only party leader who could reconcile the country. The opposition is divided because of personal and individual ambitions, and ethnic and, to a lesser extent, ideological affiliations.

CONCLUSION

Democratic discourses in Africa have started on a slippery slope. Economic crises cannot and will not advance democratic discourses. In addition, they are articulated, manipulated, and dangerously linked with primary nationalist elements like ethnicity, religion, and local cultural elements in such a way that if those forces are not critically questioned, they may become dominant in political discourse. Their absolutism can also be detrimental to any real democratic discourse. The above elements must be understood and given a different, more proper, role in the democratic struggle.

Ethnic or local nationalism is a phenomenon that can easily destroy any democracy at a national level because its philosophy is closer to religious absolutism than to secular politics. For democracy to have social meaning, political parties must socialize people and advance the concepts of human and social rights, including the right to *logos* (free speech) and life, freedom of expression and religion, respect for the law, and tolerance and appreciation of differences. All these rights must advance and protect human values individually and collectively. Democratic discourses that are separated from economic development projects and industrialization programs are socially meaningless. It does not make any sense to have the right to *logos* without a right to life. Democratic discourses must have as a main objective the improvement of the social and economic conditions for individuals and society at large. Political reforms by themselves, the introduction of multipartyism without serious economic reforms, will lead to the failure of any effort to establish a democracy. In short, political reforms should be made before economic reforms.

Another problem the struggle for democracy faces is the lack of a respectful and lawful democratic political culture within existing political parties. In Africa, individual political choice is still generally conceived as a family, clan, or even as an ethnic group matter. Government opposition and differences in political views are not easily tolerated. That is to say, democratic discourses have not yet been conceived and practiced as objective and rational discourses. One function of the political parties, both ruling parties and opposition parties, is to promote political culture through debates and collective action related to law and constructive African humanism.

Democratic discourses must be guided by an agenda and an ideal for nation-building: building a political community, rather than state-building per se. Many parties still behave as if they desire to reorganize ethnic rather than national interests. Many are not performing from the perspective of the collective consciousness. Collective interest, that is to say, the interest of the nation, must be the priority in democratic discourses. The notion of a social contract based on African consciousness and social realities must also be articulated within these discourses.

However, the African people are not necessarily or ontologically allergic to contemporary democratic discourses, procedural or substantive. For example, despite massive communication problems, legislative elections took place in Congo-Zaïre in 1965 without producing any incidence of violence in the country that had just emerged from the Congo crisis. In 1991, in Zambia and Bénin, the electoral process was realized without any serious violence. The same held true in Mali in April 1992, in Burkina Faso between January and May 1992, and in the Congo in July 1992. The local, legislative, and presidential elections in Ghana did not produce the violence that had been anticipated. The massive people's participation in the legislative and presidential elections between April 25 and 29 of 1994 in South Africa also show how this country has legitimatized multiparty democracy. In Malawi, in May 1994, multiparty elections were held unexpectedly without much violence. In short, despite intrigue and violent actions perpetrated by some internal political forces and parties, with discipline and determination, the African people can firmly decide to choose their leaders democratically. The political parties have the responsibility to advance African societies toward the creation of democratic rules and institutions. The democratic society must be conceived as an ideal society, superior to other forms of governance.

The targets for the opposition parties must be the state's public policies, its mechanisms of allocation and distribution of resources, its value system, and its ideologies, not individuals or personalities (though it may be difficult to disassociate personal actions from the institutions in which they function). Opposition parties must act lawfully to give a good example of the new leadership that is needed for the promotion of democracy. Political parties, like national institutions, should be separated from the state. They should be equipped with the necessary tools for policy analysis and political evaluation. Their actions must be predictable.

Many attempts at democracy have already occurred in Africa, but they did not succeed due to a multiplicity of factors, among which the most important are the lack of a democratic political culture in many cases, the confusion between democracy and multipartyism (an alien form of democracy that did not fit the African culture but was imposed de facto or forced in some cases), and the fact that economic reforms preceded political reforms.

Africa's greatest hope is the establishment of real social democracy and decentralized power systems to give people a chance to think about themselves, reorganize their systems of production and consumption, promote their culture and their history, and think internationally, yet act locally. However, democracy originating from the state tends to be exclusive. This exclusivity is reflected in the behavior and structures of political opposition groups. Popular participation in both state affairs and nation-building is the *sine quanon* for progress in Africa. A true democracy is one where conditions can be set for the promotion of a viable and progressive nation through individual and collective actions.

To avoid unwanted and unnecessary civil wars, unpredictable military interventions (or the return of the military to power) and secessionist movements, all political forces in African countries, including state and governments must incorporate democratic discourses into public policies and development projects. This can be done in multiparty systems as well as in one-party systems. Political parties should not function as religious organizations with their members having irrational convictions about them. Their actions must be verifiable and testable in public domains and social policies. The rationality of political parties is made up of their ability to bargain, based on their platforms, their vision of the society to be realized, and their consistency in political behavior and actions. They also should be accountable. A political party that will not bargain becomes a religious organization, incapable of entering into a broader social discourse. Absolutism of any religion does not allow for the creation of a common social base for growth and progress. The search for some form of social contract, and general transformational paradigm or objective is one of the *raisons d'être* of political parties, including the opposition ones. The social contract and the consensus has to emerge from the bottom up.

Given the nature of current philosophical and ideological contradictions in African institutions and development models and the seriousness of the African economic crisis, democratic discourses that come with different options and choices must deal with poverty elimination and political realism rather than poverty alleviation and individualistic development approaches. It is only through massive coalitions of social and political forces with continental transformational objectives that poverty can be dealt with effectively and globally. The need for the vanguard party, movement, and state is still vital. Coalitions of progressive people, parties, and movements can advance the cause of real democracy in Africa. They should play the role of political educators.

As long as opposition parties lack clear ideologies, they will continue to articulate incoherent and self-interested policies that will not collectively mobilize people's views and interests. The petty bourgeois opposition has been essentially exclusive and anti-peasants. Yet peasants and farmers are composed of more than 50 percent of the population in most parts of Africa. Imitating European opposition parties and their civil societies, but not functioning under European infrastructures and political institutions, petty bourgeois opposition parties seem to be dysfunctional, irrelevant, and powerless to challenge the ruling parties and link themselves with the people. Opposition parties without any vision or a clear ideological base are likely, if they succeed in capturing power, to fail to address people's demands with confidence. Current African conditions require that opposition parties be philosophically progressive, imaginative, lawful, and culturally sensitive in order to challenge the undemocratic practices of the ruling parties and the states.

NOTES

1.   Jacques Mariel Nzouankeu, "The Role of the National Conference in the Transition to Democracy in Africa: The Cases of Bénin and Mali," *Issue: A Journal of Opinion*, 21: 1–2 (1993): 44.

2.   To borrow Immanuel Wallerstein's definition, an antinomy between state and society involves a permanent tension, a permanent misfit or contradiction, a permanent disequilibrium. See *The World Politics of the World Economy: The States, the Movements and the Civilizations* (New York: Cambridge University Press, 1984), p. 175.

3.   "What has NDA achieved?" *Sudan Democratic Gazette* 28 (September 1992): 5.

4.   Michael Chege, "The Kenya December 1992 General Elections: Opposition Leaders Play into the Hands of the Ruling Kanu Party," *CODESRIA Bulletin* 1 (1993): 10.

5.   Tukumbi Lumumba-Kasongo, "Katangan Secessionist Movement, Manifestation of the Western Interests or Internal Power Struggle?" *Journal of African Studies* 15: (Fall/ Winter 1988–89) 3–4 .

6.   Professor Francis Wodié is the general secretary of the *Parti Ivoirien du Travail* (PIT). He was the only representative of his party in the parliament until 1995. He lost that seat in the 1995 legislative election. He is the former dean of the School of law at the National University of Abidjan. He has two *agrégations* (teaching diplomas) and is a well-known constitutionist scholar.

7.   Tukumbi Lumumba-Kasongo, "State, Economic Crisis, and Educational Reform in Côte d'Ivoire," in *Understanding Educational Reform in Global Context: Economy, State, and Ideology*, ed. Mark B. Ginsburg (New York: Garland, 1991).

8.   "FPI-PDCI: Même combat," *MDS Info* 6 (August 7, 1991): 1.

9.   Ibid.

10. Henry Bienen, "Leaders, Violence, and the Absence of Change in Africa," *Political Science Quarterly* no. 2 108 (Summer 1993): 280.

11. Ibid.

12. Cocody is one of the luxurious *communes* ("districts") of Abidjan. The active and productive members who inhabit it are mostly middle class citizens and university students.

13. Francis Wodié, "Problématique de la transition démocratique en Afrique" (Paper presented at the Seventh General Assembly of CODESRIA, Dakar, Senegal, 10–14 February 1992): p. 2.

14. Ibid., p. 16.

15. Ibid., p. 13.

16. "Faites connaissance avec le MDS" (A document of the MDS for advertising its objectives, 1992).

17. The speech of Henri Konan Bédié (speech delivered at the first opening session of the National Assembly [Parliament] of Côte d'Ivoire, April 29, 1992), p. 14 . The author was invited to attend this ceremony.

4

The Role of the Church in Democratic Pluralism in Africa

INTRODUCTION: GENERAL ISSUES

In a book that analyzes the complexity of multiparty democracy and the search for social progress, an examination of the nature and function of civil society can provide valuable information about the degree of multipartyism in a given society. The relations between civil society, society at large, and the state are complex because in principle each domain should be independent from the others, and at the same time, each has to have a special operational interaction with the others. Each should have a different mission. As Larry Diamond states:

Civil society is conceived here as the realm of organized social life that is voluntary, self-generating, (largely) self-supporting, autonomous from the state, and bound by a legal order or set of shared rules. It is distinct from "society" in general in that it involves citizens acting collectively in a public sphere to express their interests, passions, and ideas, exchange information, achieve mutual goals, make demands on the state, and hold state officials accountable.[1]

Despite the fact that civil society has historically acquired a certain degree of autonomy from the state and also has its own space, it developed in Europe, not as a parallel system to the state, but rather as part of the dynamics of the state in its relationship to the means of production. As Axelos has explained:

Civil society embraces the whole material intercourse of individuals within a definite stage of the development of productive forces. It embraces the whole commercial and industrial life of a given stage and, insofar, transcends the State and the nation, though, on the other hand again, it must assert itself in foreign relations as nationality, and inwardly must organize itself as State. The word "civil" society emerged in the eighteenth century, when property relationships had already extracted themselves from the ancient and medieval community society. Civil society as such only develops with the bourgeois; the social organization evolving directly out of production and commerce, which in all ages forms the basis of the State. (Axelos, 1976, 91)

The church is an integral part of civil society *par excellence*. Where democratic pluralism has been resisted by the state, an examination of institutionalized religion as an important force in civil society, especially in a transitional Africa, because African people are deeply religious by nature. The church is considered to be a vital cultural phenomenon. Although economics, culture, and politics are highly interrelated in real life, culture, way of life, and spirituality may be closer to human beings than other societal factors.

To understand African people one also needs to look at how they relate to, or are affiliated with, a given religion, and how they interpret the metaphysics of that religion. Every religious organization is a social force, an institution that provides values. In religion people celebrate supernatural manifestations and spiritualism. Religion has the potential of provoking change or maintaining the status quo. If appropriately mobilized by politically conscious people, it can provide the basis for social progress and the establishment of different forms of democracy. Thus, it should be analyzed as a potential social and political force. Are churches fighting only to acquire power, or do they also desire to pursue democracy, human rights, social justice, and political participation based on their ethos, or morality? What kind of social forces do churches represent? It should be noted that churches have not reacted similarly to the policies and the behavior of states. Their behavior has varied, depending on the historical, sociological, and political context in which they have been functioning.

A new popular phenomenon in most parts of Africa is the explosion of religious expressions, organizations, and movements, especially through missionary Christianity and independent churches. In urban settings, especially among the middle classes, religion has become a powerful instrument for socialization—the basis for social relations. The visibility and activism of churches in social and political affairs cannot be denied. The question is, What kind of visibility and activism? The number of churches and church members is increasing, especially in urban centers. Churches in general, and the Catholic church in particular, have played an interesting role in political activism in Africa. Since the colonial period, the Catholic church has been associated with *la mission civilisatrice* or "social progress." In the 1990s, in countries such as Côte d'Ivoire, Bénin, Congo, Kenya, Malawi, Togo, and Congo-Zaïre, church leaders have taken controversial positions regarding general social conditions in their countries. For instance, in March 1992, Malawi's Roman Catholic bishops defied existing traditions by publicly attacking the government for human rights abuses and calling for democracy in a highly critical pastoral letter.[2] Their declarations were controversial if the content of their message and the classical mission of churches are compared. In Liberia, for instance, the Liberian Council of Churches (LCC) attempted to mediate outstanding political differences after Doe's inauguration as president in 1986, even though Doe had persecuted members of the LCC.[3] Before his retirement from the *apostolat* in early 1995, the late Cardinal Yago of Côte d'Ivoire strongly criticized the *Parti Démocratique de la Côte d'Ivoire* (PDCI), the ruling party, for not promoting human rights and for imprisoning opposition party leaders as a result of a mass demonstration in early February 1992. As indicated earlier, the demonstrators turned to mob violence. Much physical damage was orchestrated in downtown Abidjan, including setting cars on fire and breaking into offices.

Since 1982, in Kenya, the criticism against the one-party state and Moi's dictatorship was intensified by the Catholic bishops, the Protestant National Council of Churches of Kenya (NCCK) and the Presbyterian Church of East Africa. The Catholic bishops' pastoral letters in 1991 against the emergence of a South American-style caudillo dictatorship, complete with torture and death squads, and the letter of April 1992 in which Moi was informed that he was extremely unpopular and that the public had lost faith in him, are some examples of the Catholic church's positions in Kenya.[4]

Catholic cardinals and bishops participate in national conferences in Bénin, the Congo, Togo, and Congo-Zaïre, to cite only a few countries. Several have been presidents of the national conferences. However, what is not clear is both the nature of their protests and the definition of their concept of democracy, as well as the kind of society the Catholic church wants or is inclined to continue to promote. What is the basis of legitimacy for the churches to be involved in this political activism?

The selection of the Catholic church as part of this analysis is more or less personal and random. At the same time, in recent years, Catholic church leaders have led national political debates in Africa. This church is a social factor that should be critically analyzed and understood. It has a large constituency that should be taken into account. Within the context of the emergence of religious fundamentalism within both Islam and Christianity as well as in popular movements, this chapter on the role of the Catholic church in Zaire sheds some light on the complexity of studying multiparty politics, social protest, and the search for social progress.

Social protest and power struggle are the major forces through which the claims for state power have been actualized within a given social class or administrative structure of neo-colonial politics in Africa. Regardless of the nature of social protests, modernization theorists, especially American functionalist and neo-functionalist sociologists, and political scientists like Apter, Huntington, Lapalombra, and Parsons, claimed in the past that social protests are essentially irrational actions that can impede institutional stability (for instance, state-building). Consequently, they are antithetical to social change in developing countries. Some scholars have perceived social protests as acts that support and advance atavistic, popular, and utopian demands that do not reflect the structures of the world system and are unrealistic and primordial. These theorists have generalized about social protests and thus lack true understanding of the history and politics of social protest, its origins, and its dynamism.

Some advocates of modernization have reduced social protest to the level of psychologism or behaviorism of anti-institutionalism or of anti-legalism; that is to say, at the level of emotion, irrationality, and unpredictability. This book argues that the objectives of social protest, as expressed by institutions or social groups, should be concretely analyzed within the context of the relations between the role of protesters within the hierarchy of power and the structures of political economy in their given social milieu. As one attempts to examine this phenomenon, the social context in which protests occur, the history of a given social protest, and the nature of protesters must be taken seriously. Social protests are not ends unto themselves. They are directed against different forms of power domination and injustice. They are teleologically instrumental. Who are the actors involved in this struggle? What are their objectives?

Social protest is based on a certain level of social, religious, or political crisis within a given social milieu or social class. Every crisis embodies both construction and de-construction. Any social protest agenda embodies a project. A social protest's ideology is more important than its behavior because it can help depict the nature of its project and inform us why protesters behave the way they do.

For different reasons, various movements or institutions, including the Catholic church, have protested against the illegitimacy of the African state and policies and its social injustices (the results of the implementation of those policies). Various social classes have challenged one another to acquire state power—not necessarily because of their ideological differences, but rather because of their in-class basis and claims, and disagreements concerning various policies and political issues. In many cases, the lack of consensus among the "elite" has led to power struggle. Not all protest movements are conservative, progressive or revolutionary. Not all protest movements act to maintain the status quo or bring about radical change in a given society. The Catholic church, not being a movement, has used a different institutional basis for making its public statement. What is the nature of this basis? Since the 1960s the church has been visible in social and political affairs in Africa. The Fulbert Youlous (Youlou was a Catholic priest, who became the first president of Congo-Brazzaville) have been the advocates of state nationalism.

Is it by historical coincidence or sociological accident that a multitude of churches are emerging during the intensification of underdevelopment in Africa? Can the same political and economic explanations of underdevelopment help us explain the explosive nature of the church phenomenon? What has become so attractive in church teachings and practices of late that massive numbers have joined them? One of the characteristics of neo-colonialism in Africa is the massive building of churches—both independent indigenous ones and Western missionary ones. In Ghana, Kenya, Liberia, Nigeria, Togo, Zambia, and Congo-Zaïre, churches are mushrooming, competing with the development of underdevelopment. Also, many have been informally competing with ruling political parties in member recruitment. Church "charlatans" are everywhere.

Until recently, churches were among the few public arenas where members expected to express themselves with a certain degree of freedom about state policies and societal structures. In Africa, most public places are not restricted in terms of access use. The public market place has also become the meeting place for many churchgoers and their prophets to publicize their messages. Though the demographics of Christians are proportionately increasing in relation to population growth in many regions of Africa, Christianity is not the dominant continental religion in absolute terms, as many Western scholars of religion have claimed in their studies of missionary work. The major question is: Why is it that the quality of the church's message and organizational structure have not yet produced massive social protests in Africa, as they tend to claim? What positive role have African churches played in fighting political dictatorship and underdevelopment? A theoretical perspective is needed to clarify some generalized assumptions.

Karl Marx, a critic of social and productive relations, defined religion as the "opium" of the people. It creates illusions for the poor and support systems for the structure and values of more powerful classes. It pacifies weaker social classes and promotes dogmas used to demand respect for authority. It advances the notion of a good life in the kingdom of God, relegating the pursuit of secular social justice to the domain of the temporal world. In this sense, it alienates people from their social origins and history. However, Marx would probably applaud the role of any church that could become a modernizing agent, producing workers who could build social institutions or infrastructures of capitalism. A church that can organize its members, raise their consciousness, and challenge the secular powers in the world system with a concrete social agenda can be considered a modernizer. Its follows that internal contradictions within this world system, as reflected in local political and economic structures, would advance the revolution and class struggle. Marx saw religion as an ideology of the powerful classes or an instrument of domination *par excellence*. In Europe, especially in the medieval period, the church was on the side of secular power. In many parts of Europe, it was once the only ruling power. The pope was once the head of state. The Holy Roman Empire represented both supernatural and natural powers.

Today, although the number of people attending church services on Sundays has drastically dropped in some European countries such as France, Christian values are still central in their societies. What does all this mean within the context of colonial and neo-colonial situations in Africa? An analysis of a concrete case of Catholic church in Congo-Zaïre can answer this question. Congo-Zaïre was chosen because of the special role the church in this country played in the colonization process and post-colonial politics. This role can be generalizable. To understand the current role of the Catholic church in Congo-Zaïre, it is necessary to analyze it within the dynamism of both national and international politics.

THE CATHOLIC CHURCH AND POLITICS IN CONGO-ZAÏRE

It is not by accident that Monsignor Mossengwo Passinya was chosen as a compromising person to be the chairperson of the national conference in 1992. In October 1995 he was accused of being a Mobutuist by the radical opposition in the transitional parliament and forced to resign. On May 10, 1997, he was re-elected as the chairperson of the transitional parliament, under obscure circumstances, as the Alliance of the Democratic Forces for the Liberation of the Congo (ADFLC) continued to advance towards Kinshasa, and Mobutu continued to reinforce his military might in the city with French, Serbian, and UNITA forces. This time, however, he did not accept the post. While Mossengwo Passinya was about to start the process of consulting with various political forces in Kinshasa, the ADFLC took over power in Kinshasa on May 16, 1997. However, the point that he did not come from an obscure social environment and hierarchy of power in Congo-Zaïre is still relevant in the context of the analysis in this book.

The role that the Catholic church has played in the colonization and de-colonization process, and the consolidation policies of the neo-colonial state in Congo-Zaïre, have produced a unique political experience in African politics. The separation of church and state in other former African colonies, in the French, Portuguese and British systems for example, left room for possible political conflicts between church and state leaders. Ever since the Congo Free State (1885–1908), the Catholic church has not been a passive observer in the process of state-building and underdevelopment in Congo-Zaïre. It had a mandate to educate, Christianize, and so-called civilize Africans, and it signed a pact with King Léopold II to do just that. Beginning in 1909, the Congo was ruled by the trinity of the Belgian State, the Catholic church, and private corporations. Based on the practices of the colonial state, and the interactions between these three forces, the Catholic church was a de facto state religion. In many local districts, *chefferies* (small prefects), or mission stations, fathers, brothers, and sisters represented the state in local political disputes. They occasionally helped the colonial administration collect taxes as well. Before the 1948 educational reforms, when Protestant churches were also given official recognition for their participation in education, the Catholic church was the only authority in education. This made the Congo-Zaïrean political and social experience different from other colonial experiences in Africa.

In comparison with colonial state, which was only the powerful force of domination and savage exploitation, the Catholic church played the role of an agent of enlightenment, with a narrow colonial context. It educated masses of people and African *évolués* ("evolved" used here as elite). It helped create clubs or organizations that later became the foundations for political formations. What kind of education did it provide? What were the major goals of such an education?

As already stated, one of the objectives in this chapter is to examine the role of the Catholic church in Zaïre in the protest movement and the search for democracy between 1960 and 1997. Some of the questions included in this section are: What kind of protest agent has the church been? What are the characteristics of this protest and its underlying ideology? What kind of society and human beings does it intend to create? In short, what were the relations between church, state, and society like in the period under study? Although this book historically analyzes the general objectives of the Catholic church in Congo-Zaïre, especially in the education, it focuses on the role of the church as a protest force in post-colonial politics and society in Congo-Zaïre. How does the church perceive the neo-colonial state? What were its reactions to the processes of Mobutuist state-building and public policy formation?

In using historical-structural paradigms with an emphasis on policies, this book is particularly interested in the structures of power in the church and their relationship to the struggle for democracy. Though philosophical and theological references are not used as the basis for the argument that the church has been advancing, this work is not exegetic (or hermeneutic). Its emphasis is on the political and sociological implications of the role of the church within the context of underdevelopment in Congo-Zaïre. Protest movements and institutions cannot operate without a certain level of anger and disagreement. The church is not a social movement, but it has posed some acts against the state. Church and state relations illustrate the basis for this anger and disagreement.

In studying the Catholic church as an agent of social protest or a conspirator in the power struggle in Congo-Zaïre, two schools of thought dominate. There are those who say that the Catholic church has always been part of the colonial empire and has behaved accordingly. It has exploited Africans by destroying their cultural basis, forcing them to adopt Christianity by using totalitarian and authoritarian methods, and pacifying them in order to pave the way for commercial and social exploitative practices that were actualized by the state and corporations. Its message for Christianizing Africans is another expression for westernizing Africans. Regardless of the nature of the political discourses that took place after the independence of the Congo, the Catholic church struggled to preserve its role as a saviour and educator of Western ideas and culture. That is to say, the conflict between church and state in the post-colonial Congo is viewed as a power struggle. This power struggle is based on the proclaimed historical legitimacy of the church. From this perspective, this church was not likely to promote democracy.

There are others who think that the Catholic church in the Congo has always played the role of enlightenment and philanthropy. It has taken its official mission seriously by serving the people, combating social injustices, and preaching equality and respect for human values. As a universal church, it is convinced that the truth it preaches is also universal. Because formal education was under the control and responsibility of the church, its contribution here has been considerable. It built the first institutions of higher education and trained the first generation of African *évolués*. In the face of policies that led to social atrocities and mal-development (inappropriate development) projects, the church felt obligated to protest state policies. Here the conflict between the Catholic church and the state may be considered the struggle between spiritual educator and secular power. The church protests to bring about moral and social changes in people's lives and provides a new sense of direction to the community of believers. Here democracy can be seen as one of its values.

The above positions are analyzed from a historical perspective with special attention to their policy implications. It is argued that by the nature of the Catholic church, its structures of hierarchy of power, its direct relations with the Vatican, a metropolitan foreign power dominated by Western culture and politics, and its historical connections with colonial powers in the Congo, its social protest approach could not be transformed into a national revolutionary dogma and real social democracy. At the same time, until recently, the Catholic church has been the most outspoken institution against the behavior and policies of the Mobutu regime. The question is: What is the ideological base for this social protest? The Catholic church in the Congo has played a complex role as an agent of social protest, but it has proved to be incapable of preaching a message of comprehensive social change similar to that of the South American theology of liberation. Can this church disassociate itself from its hierarchy of power and its cultural basis of power and make the necessary popular social protest statement for the establishment of democracy in Africa?

THE CATHOLIC CHURCH AS AN EDUCATOR

Some questions to pose are: What kind of educator has the Catholic church been in Zaïre? What were its political objectives in pursuing its educational mission? What kind of society is embodied in the philosophy of this educational mission— a democratic society or a submissive one?

As previously mentioned, the Belgian policy of education was based on the *pas d'élite pas de problème* ("no elite, no problem") conception. Education, especially higher education, was perceived as a potentially dangerous intellectual, social, and political phenomenon. This conception shaped colonial politics and the so-called civilizing mission of the Belgian administration. As is indicated elsewhere in book, until the educational and political reforms of 1948, the colonial administration considered education to be a threatening force. What in the content of education was perceived as threatening to the structure of the colonial empire? In any case, a massive primary education was promoted for Africans.

The Catholic church in the Congo was part of the official colonial power structure. The Church signed a contract with Léopold II to undertake the responsibility of colonial education. In this capacity the Catholic church, in its role of educator, directly represented the interests and ideologies of the dominant classes. It was the transmitter of European culture and civilization and the destroyer of African culture and civilization. All these dimensions were reflected not only in the behavior of the Catholic missionaries, but in the content of what was taught and the structures of their institutions as well.

Despite the contradictory nature of the Catholic church's role, it provided an education that was used later as an instrument of political struggle. As Joseph Kizerbo indicates, despite the nature of the education provided by the colonial administration (*éducation tronquée* ["truncated education"] as he called it), it became an autonomous and incoercible force in itself (1972). He believes that any education as a learning process can transcend its own social conditions to create its own struggle to pave the way for social change; even without being totally a liberated tool, education as it deals with mind and body has the potential to provoke discourses that can lead to power struggle or social movements.

Before the 1947 and 1948 reforms, Catholic education had two main objectives: to teach Africans how to read the Bible or *catéchisme* to foster respect for the new authority and law and order, and to provide corporations and states with workers without critical thinking skills who would be satisfied with their material conditions. For these purposes, the emphasis was put on primary education and technical vocational education. The mass primary education was promoted in the Belgium Congo. It concentrated on Christian moral dogma and its political and social implications—an education that supported the policy of *pas d'élite pas de problème* promoted by the state. Ruth M. Slade states:

Theoretically the evolution of Zaïre was to have taken place in a logical succession of the slow and easy stages; mass education to provide a literate population. Before education elite was considered and long apprenticeship in consultative councils. It was to prepare the way for democratic institutions at some remote date. At the same time, as a system of social welfare and (gradually) of the African middle class it provided satisfaction for the immediate future, and it was thought that a calm peaceful discussion of economic and political emancipation could safely be relegated to some distant period. (1960, 11)

The high demand for workers (especially in the mines and plantations), political pressures from power and ideological struggles in Brussels between progressive and conservative parties, the continuation of social protests from local forces, the emergence of nationalist movements in other African countries, and the coming to power of Buisseret as the governor-general,[5] created a social environment for change. Buisseret introduced in 1948 the classical secondary schools. The aim was to ensure good training that would permit students to gain better jobs and to prepare a few selected students for university education; the main objective was to encourage the presence of an elite from which it would be possible to choose those who were not only intellectually but also morally fit to receive and benefit from superior training. The newly created schools were divided into *Gréco-Latines* which emphasized the liberal arts, and *humanités modernes*, which emphasized mathematics, physics, biology and chemistry. Requirements for admission into those schools included:

1. A successful primary school examination.
2. A certificate of good conduct (and for church related schools, a certificate of baptism).
3. A recommendation from the local authorities to ensure that the student had been loyal to the colonial administration. In those schools, reason, good behavior, and faith in Christianity were the most important criteria for succeeding.

Until 1954, the only place where Congolese could acquire a complete post-primary and secondary education was in the Catholic seminaries. *Séminaires Petits* were the equivalent of the classical secondary system, and *grands séminaires* provided the post-secondary education, where the emphasis was on classical philosophy, Christian history and theology, oratory, and some limited history of philology and ethnology. Only a selected few high achievers and "morally good" students, based on the Catholic code of laws and behavior were admitted into seminaries. These schools became a means for social mobility and personal achievement.

In 1947, the Catholic church created a medical and agricultural training center known as the first *Centre Universitaire Congolais* at Kisantu near its well-known Grand Séminaire. It was sponsored by the *Université de Louvain* in Brussels and its *Centre Agronomique* ("Agricultural Center"). Although the center did not confer degrees until the 1950s, the programs were oriented toward a progressive elevation of the vocational school systems to make them more equivalent for universities. In 1954 the Université Lovanium was inaugurated in Léopoldville (capital of the Congo). The programs of this Catholic university included a strong department of theology, not inferior to those in European universities. Its curriculum was the same as that of the Université de Louvain in Brussels, and most of its staff and faculty were recruited directly from Belgium. Only a few Africans were admitted into this school. Among them, especially those admitted into Pre-Université (Pre-U) none were allowed to graduate until the early 1960s. Until 1959, enrollment was dominated by Europeans. In fact, this university was not established for Africans. It was part of the long-term agenda of the colonial power, which in the 1950s planned to remain in the Congo 80 more years.

The teachings and philosophy of education in the Université Lovanium and the *grand séminaire* reflect the kind of African society embodied in the agenda of the Catholic church. This society should be embedded in Christian dogma. The elite should be highly selective and separated from the rest of society by privileges and education. The basis for this new bourgeoisie would not be materialism, but rather reason and faith. *Séminaristes* were versed in Latin and Greek, the teachings of Saint Augustine, Thomas Aquina, and other church fathers, but they understood very little about what was politically happening in and around their own country. That is to say, this education made them apolitical. Morality rather than political consciousness was considered the correct basis for making social requests. African value systems were supposed to be abandoned. The model of society to be imitated in the future was the European one. This logic presented an intellectual contradiction regarding the *déontologie* and of state's policy, which emphasized that Africans could not even be like Belgians in behavior and thought. They were considered incapable of imitating Europeans. In addition, *séminaristes* were trained in the universalist philosophy of Christianity. Yet the state did not believe in the universalization of Congolese conditions and productive forces. The Belgian ruling class believed that Congo was unique and that it could remain unique and isolated from other colonial experiences in Africa. There was a conflict between the universalist nature of Catholic teachings and the politics of the state which refused to see the implications of capitalism in local African conditions. This church produced the large majority of the African elite in Zaïre.

Though limited in its scope, the role that the elite played in the formation of political organizations and the political struggles for the independence of the Congo cannot be underestimated. Social and political conditions in the country did not produce radical political figures comparable in stature to Kwame Nkrumah, Ahmed Sékou Touré, Nasser, Modibo Kéita, Nelson Mandela, and Félix Houphouët-Boigny. *Evolués* like Patrice Lumumba came into African political scene later. However, the belief of the colonial power that Congo was unique case politically was inconsistent and historically anachronistic. There was an elite class that was consciously formed to fulfill certain tasks within the colonial administration. Its mission was essentially to prevent revolutionary situations from occurring in the Congo. They had to maintain the status quo. This mission was complex. This class lacked the power and political ability to pose decolonization issues and political questions; but at same time, it had high expectations as to what it should do, and how it wished to integrate the European power structure. As Buisseret says:

We must organize a class of natives évolués, who will declare their acceptance of ideals and the principles of our civilization and who will be on an equal standing with us, our equal in rights, and duties. Less numerous than the masses, but powerful and influential, they will be indispensable allies in the native communities. These middle classes will be the black bourgeoisie that is beginning to develop everywhere, which like all the bourgeoisies of the world, will be opposed to any disruption, internal or external.[6]

In 1959, there were about 11,500 individuals classified as évolués, of whom more than 70 percent were trained in Catholic church schools or Catholic-affiliated schools, including medical and agricultural institutes and seminaries. Many of them were anciens prêtres ("former priests"). In general these évolués, especially those who acquired philosophical and theological training were far from being organic intellectuals in Gramci's sense, that is members of a social body that sees its role in a given society as that of an agent of political change or a critic of politics. Wamba-dia-Wamba characterizes intellectuals among the Congolese elite as functionaries of the sophisticated catechists, that is militant propagandists of dominant, essentially Western, ideas about Africans and thus unable to give to African societies their (proper) image.[7]

Political organizations were formed along ethnic and religious lines. Many political parties started as cultural associations in urban areas. Anciens élèves ("former students") grouped themselves by a common idealism to advance their political views. Thus, many Catholic students and intellectuals were highly visible in the early political debates in the Congo. The late Cardinal Albert Malula was among the Catholic priests who actively participated in the political negotiations representing the évolués and the colonial power. For instance, Joseph Kasavubu, the first president of the Republic of Congo, strongly represented his Catholicism in national politics, though he also hoped to become the leader of the unified Bakongo ethnic group. In general, however, the church did not support the radical national political tendencies represented by nationalists such as Patrice Lumumba through his Mouvement National Congolais/Lumumba (MNC/L). It supported the ideological tendencies of the late President (abbé) Fulbert Youlou of the Congo-Brazzaville (formerly the People's Republic of the Congo and also a formerly French colony), who was a former Catholic priest who had been very close to the Catholic leaders in Léopoldville (Congo-Kinshasa). He was the only head of state in the Congo-Brazzaville who until recently did not have any formal association with socialist movements, ideologies, or labor unions.

The Catholic church, however, was involved in the decolonization process by attempting to Africanize some aspects of the church: for instance, using African songs and other local references in church liturgies. Its actions cannot be characterized as symbols of protest. On the contrary, its efforts can be viewed as one of continuously working toward integrating the Congolese Catholic church into the larger family of world Catholics and Western culture. The hierarchical structures of power in the Church were not questioned. Moreover, other ways of thinking or believing were not tolerated. This intolerance has been a source of much conflict between Africans and the church.

THE CATHOLIC CHURCH IN POST-COLONIAL POLITICS

The Catholic church enjoyed privileges associated with state power even after the independence of the Congo, especially as most of the new political leaders were themselves members of this church. It was a state in a state like the Mining Corporation called the *Union Minière du Haut Katanga*. The first time that the church started to openly disagree with the state was after Joseph-Désiré Mobutu came to power on November 24, 1965 by a military coup d'état. Mobutu had the support of the Catholic church when he first came into power. He was a Catholic, though there is no convincing evidence that he was faithfully a practicing one. Some scholars suggest that the sources of conflict between Church and state can be found on the following grounds:

1. Personality differences between Mobutu and the late Cardinal Malula (the former leader of the Catholic church)
2. The process of state power consolidation as a means of Congolization or Zaïreanization
3. The deterioration of social, political, and economic conditions in the country.

In 1967, before the promotion of "authenticity," in the charter of the *Mouvement Populaire de la Révolution* (MPR), the N'Sele Manifesto (inspired by the green book of Gaddafi of Libya and the red book of Mao) it is stated that: "The Congo has known religious oppression, and this still exists as long as philosophic or religious conceptions are imposed on it."[8] From that year to the present, the relations between church and state have gradually deteriorated. The Catholic church has clearly articulated its position through its annual episcopal meetings and special meetings of church leaders. These positions were made public in the form of open letters to the Zaïrean authorities, especially to Mobutu. The nature of the military regime has made conflict inevitable.

The confrontation between them became more acute in October 1971 when Mobutu and his party the MPR vigorously launched their campaign of authenticity. Mobutu claimed that authenticity meant the search for African values and culture, as is stated in a special note in *Pro Mundi Vita:*

The idea of authenticity helps the Zaïrians to get over a certain trauma that was created by the colonial epoch. They have derived from it the aspiration and resolve to be themselves, something which was never the case during the colonial period when everything was judged by reference to the Whites. President Mobutu with his usual eloquence expressed this clearly in one of his speeches to the masses. "We are now embarking on our cultural liberation, the quest of our African, Zaïrian soul. We men of black skin have had imposed on us the mentality of quite a different race. We must become once more authentic Africans, authentic blacks, authentic Zaïrians."[9]

Despite the inconsistency and contradictions in the politics and policy implications of authenticity, it clearly became a serious challenge to the dogmas, power structure, and political history of the Catholic church in Zaïre. The campaign of authenticity was global and carried out by individuals from all social classes. It was felt the most in the educational system.

In fiscal year 1972–73 the percentages of students enrolled in Catholic schools was 61.7 at the primary level and 42.1 at the secondary level.[10] The nationalization of the schools had a significant impact on an educational system that had been controlled by the Catholic church until that time. A summary of some major state decisions is needed to show how far the politics of authenticity attempted to go:

- All Christian names were legally dropped.
- All European names of places, streets, and monuments were replaced by African names.
- Mobutu's picture replaced that of Jesus Christ in churches and church-affiliated institutions.
- Mobutu's mother, maman Yemo, was referred to as the Virgin Mary and Mobutu himself as the prophet.
- Christian holidays were suppressed.
- Religion courses were replaced by civic education courses based on the *Manifeste de la N'Sele.*
- The *Université Lovanium* was nationalized, along with other universities.
- The John XXIII Major Seminary was closed down.
- Confessional newspapers and periodicals and Catholic radio and television services were suspended.
- The Episcopal Assembly of Zaïre was dissolved.
- Father Mosmans, secretary-general of the Episcopate of Zaïre, was expelled.
- The Saint Paul's printing plant at Kinshasa was closed down.

These are some of the actions Mobutu took against the Catholic church in the name of authenticity. Faced with these events and their implications for its survival and functioning, the church had to react. How did it react? What kind of protest did the church undertake against all this moves? In what name was the church protesting? These are some questions to guide the following discussion.

Authenticity implies some kind of decolonization of all Zaïrean institutions. This should mean their Africanization, in principle. In this Mobutu had intellectual support from some members of the faculty of theology at the *Universitté Lovanium.* This group was led by Msgr. Tshibangu Tshishiku, who was working on the issues of African theology. His position is reflected by a statement he made in the Synod of Bishops in Rome in 1974:

Africans who are conscious of the cultural values of their society and jealous of their identity are anxious to keep and safeguard their authentic personality in every domain. We want today to be authentic Christians whilst remaining at the same time authentic Africans. African generations of today want to see Christianity in its religious non-cultural form and the essence of African religion, to be found in special categories of thought, brought together. For a start, it is now recognized and admitted that there is identity of the God adored by the African peoples and the God whom the Christian apostle announces.[11]

This statement fully supports the politics and philosophy of authenticity. When higher education was nationalized, Tshibangu was named rector (the equivalent of vice chancellor within the British system or president within the U.S. system) of the former National University of Zaïre, a highly political position indeed. The statement of the late Cardinal Malula in the same synod was not essentially different from Tshibangu's statement. Malula said:

The contemporary world which has to be evangelized is for us Africans the whole of black Africa which wants to be itself, free from all forms of mental alienation. It is to this Africa that we have to announce Jesus Christ as Lord and Saviour of man, in his political, economic, cultural and spiritual aspects. It is not for us to judge the evangelization of Africa carried out by foreign missionaries. The past is past. We must look resolutely to the future and see how the Church in Africa is to be indigenized, made local, in order to bear authentic witness to Jesus Christ. This task falls in the first place to African Christians. It demands a deep sense of responsibility, creativity and dynamism.[12]

Although they did not consider policy implications of authenticity in their approach, it is clear that at first both Tshibangu and Malula were on the side of state power concerning the essence of the philosophy or ideology of authenticity. What was the basis of the protest of the Catholic church against the state?

Between 1971 and 1975, a series of negotiations were undertaken between church and state on the effects of the politics of authenticity. Protest was expressed through *lettres pastorales* ("Pastoral letters"), which were also made public. The one published on January 5, 1975 by Msgr. Bakole, Archbishop of Kananga, for example, was among the most publicized documents. Major ideas of this pastoral letter can be summarized in his statement:

Let us now therefore think that the Church can only exist on the model of a great institution such as we have known it up to now in this country of ours. This difficulty is that we are not used to this more informal, more spontaneous manner of being a Church. Starting from an organization which is directed by clerics we must press for a movement from below, a popular movement. We must de-institutionalize our pastoral work and find the Church on a much smaller scale, that of grass-roots communities. We are convinced that man (or the nation) becomes very dangerously alienated, loses his liberty and his dignity, and fails in his responsibility when he binds himself to any kind of idol, or when he absolutizes or divinizes a man or a human institution.[13]

The call for a popular movement by a Catholic leader is in itself very much a revolutionary action. This new dimension was added to the process of protest. Other pastoral letters, including the one signed by 47 bishops under Chairman of council of bishops, Msgr. Lesambo Ndamwize on January 15, 1975 emphasized the mission of the church and its relationship with the Universal church as a community of faith and to the temporal world.

De-Zaïreanization was due to the failure of the state to perform efficiently and productively in all sectors of the economy. Thus, the World Bank and the International Monetary Fund (IMF) recommended privatization of state agencies through their Structural Adjustment Programs (SAPs). They were interested in creating conditions in which the state could become more efficient and regular in paying off its loans. This brought new dynamics to the protest agenda.

In the 1970s the acts of protests were more doctrinal. They were articulated on the basis of the fundamental moral premises of the Catholic church. As social, economic, and political conditions continued to worsen in the 1980s, the voice of the Catholic church also became more radical. It became more direct and sounded more political. In numerous pastoral letters, the Zaïrean sickness and its social consequences (for instance, corruption, underdevelopment, mismanagement, and the implications of the politics of authenticity) were identified and attacked. As the opposition against the Mobutu regime grew in the whole society, the Catholic church continued to raise issues concerning the absolutist nature of the regime. The issue of the lack of democracy and fundamental human liberties became the center of its discourse.

At the end of 1989 and in early 1990, the voices of popular movements, such as those of market women, students, public servants, and the lumpen-proletariat, asked for Mobutu's resignation. By that time, social tensions had nearly reached the level of explosion. Mobutu called for a so-called national debate on the question of the origin of the mal-Zaïrois ("Zaïrean malady") and what should be done. The Catholic bishops sent the strongest letter that had ever been written by any group to Mobutu. They also made the letter public. Bishops testified about social conditions in Zaïre and requested that action be taken to alleviate poverty and prevent the destruction of more souls. The tone of the letter and its content clearly reflect their disagreements with the regime.

Political reforms and the birth of the Third Republic that Mobutu announced on April 25, 1990 were partially due to pressures he had received over two decades from various groups, the most important being the Catholic church. Political parties have mushroomed in Zaïre despite Mobutu's political zigzagging. He wanted to retain power by all means necessary. The Catholic church does not want to create its own political party. However, the *Parti Démocratique et Social Chrétien* (PDSC), led by Joseph Iléo, though dominated by Catholics, is also open to Protestants, Kibanguists, and members of other faiths.

The Catholic church has participated in the struggle for democracy and social change. At the same time, it has not disassociated itself from world power structures. The elitist notion of democracy most of its leaders have advocated can provoke social change. However, in the context of total social paralysis, as in Zaïre, can an elitist or bourgeois kind of democracy be desirable for the majority of the people?

CONCLUSION

Has the Catholic church in Congo-Zaïre been an agent of social protest or a conspirator in the power struggle? In post-authenticity politics, as the whole society is struggling towards the search for democracy, this institution is still one of the strongest institutions in terms of its potential to get things done and its ability to influence things. This church has been part of the structure of state power since the colonial era. The secularity of the Congolese state was clearly confirmed in the *Loi Fondamentale* (the fundamental laws) and Mobutu's constitutions, and it is likely that it will also be reflected in the new constitution of the Third Republic (the Democratic Republic of Congo). However, for pragmatic, ideological, and historical reasons, the church resists any attempts that could create a sharp separation between church and state. It wishes to continue to bring its input directly to the political governance of the country as a privileged social and religious institution.

As indicated in this chapter, the Catholic church was not against authenticity as such, but it was against the political consequences of authenticity like political absolutism and monopoly of state power. If the social conditions in Zaïre had not became intolerable and the church could have continued to relatively enjoy its privileges as it had in the past, it would probably not have raised its voice against the state. Was this protest based on the moral principles of the church, or is it a product of a situation that was created by state power consolidation? The top leaders of the church were related to the state apparatus. They supported the ideology of the neo-colonial state. They also received grand gifts from Mobutu. Conflict was intensified when the church saw that the state was trying to question and displace its historical role. At this level the act of protest is a manifestation of a power struggle.

For an act to be qualified as social protest, it must embody the social, economic, and political agenda of a particular social group, class, or society at a given time. In the 1970s, the Catholic church did not systematically deal with this agenda. Social issues were articulated within the general framework of the theology of power. In the 1980s and 1990s, however, this church has raised serious questions about the nature of the neo-colonial state in Zaïre, especially its inability to govern properly. However, it was not prepared to go further with Msgr. Bakole of Kananga's line of reasoning that the church should be transformed, for evangelical purposes, into a popular movement.

The political history of Zaïre testifies that the state changes its policies or its political behavior only when faced with actions advanced by popular movements. In 1959, the Belgian rulers were not immune to the people's anger, disappointment, and quest for democracy. Although the actions of the elite negotiating for independence with the Belgian administration should not be depreciated, they would not have occurred without popular movements. The efforts of the petty bourgeoisie were based on class interests, not national interests.

The Catholic church, in its efforts to protest against the state, did not ally itself with people's movements. It did not form coalitions of interests or ideologies with other social forces that were not satisfied with the performance of the state. In fact, the leaders of the Catholic church protested without directly involving members of their own congregations. Their behavior was elitist and, thus, it reduced their ability to see things in national or global terms.

The new dynamics of political pluralism have entered into the political history of Africa. Democracy is the most popular agenda. The credibility of the Catholic church will be tested in its effort to contribute to the establishment of popular and social democracy in the Democratic Republic of Congo. The Congolese society is in deep social and economic crisis, unprecedented in its contemporary history.

Under Mobutu and Mobutuism, Zaïre became the most corrupt society in Africa. The Zaïrean state produced also the most illegitimate government. To be able to productively deal with corruption and illegitimacy, the Catholic church will have to first question its own power structure. The church cannot claim to propose social actions for the benefit of the people without first becoming a people's church. Its bourgeois tendencies must be critically evaluated in light of its new responsibilities within the new political dynamism and social exigencies in the Democratic Republic of Congo. After all, Jesus Christ came to save the poor and to give freedom to oppressed peoples, not to be on the side of any state power or privileged few. As Julius Nyerere, the former president of Tanzania said:

My purpose is to suggest to you that the Church should accept that development of peoples means rebellion. At a given and decisive point in history men decide to act against those conditions which restrict their freedom as men. I am suggesting that, unless we participate actively in the rebellion against those social structures and economic organizations which condemn men to poverty, humiliation and degradation, then the Church will become irrelevant to man and the Christian religion will degenerate into a set of superstitions accepted by the fearful. Unless the Church, its members and its organizations, express God's love for man by involvement and leadership in constructive protest against the present conditions of man, then it will be identified with injustice and persecution. (1974, 85)

To continue as a critic of the state, means that the church should continue to get involved in people's projects and separate its process of actions from state structures. It is then and only then that one can adequately deal with people's needs and their political and spiritual demands. Some elements of the liberation theology of South America, revised and adopted into African conditions could be interesting intellectual, philosophical, and political possibilities for the Catholic church to deal with the illegitimacy of the Zaïrean state and the social calamities it has produced. As Father Pablo Richard says: "The Third World needs a new model of Church which responds to its own political and cultural situation. As long as the Church continues to be Western and colonial, it will never be universal."[14]

　　To contribute to the social progress of the Democratic Republic of Congo in a more productive way, the church should consider embracing the ethics of strength as the basis and motivation for its social actions. Modern politics understands and operates mainly on the premise of this ethic. The Catholic church must initiate and provide welfare services, advance and support social projects that the state fails to offer, and be on the side of the people. It is through the establishment of popular democracy that the above elements can be fully realized. It has to move away from the concentration of the power of the clergy among men and the headquarters of the Catholic church in Rome. That is to say, it has to be functionally democratic. It also has to preach respect for life and self-determination. This is the challenge for the Universal Church in the Democratic Republic of Congo in particular and in Africa in general, as we enter the era of the struggle for democracy as the *sine qua non* for African progress.

NOTES

1. Larry Diamond, "Rethinking Civil Society: Toward Democratic Consolidation," *Journal of Democracy* 5:3 (July 1994): 4.

2. Makau Wa Mutua, "Decline of the Despot," *Africa Report* (July–August 1994): 49.

3. S. Byron Tarr, "The ECOMOG Initiative in Liberia: A Liberian Perspective," *Issue: A Journal of Opinion* 21:1–2 (1993): 74.

4. For further information on this subject see Michael Chege's article entitled: "Return of Multiparty Politics," in *Beyond Capitalism Vs Socialism in Kenya and Tanzania*, ed. Joel D. Barkan (Boulder, Co: Lynne Rienner, 1994).

5. Buisseret was a progressive colonialist who firmly believed in the *mission civilisatrice* of the Belgian administration. He was convinced that this mission would fail unless the colonial power up-graded the level of education of Africans and created an elite class.

6. CRISP, "Organisation et education des colons au Congo: Fédération Congolaise des classes moyennes (FEDECOL)," *Courriers d'Afrique* 35 (July 1959): 67–68.

7. Wamba-dia-Wamba, "African Intellectuals and Philosophy," Paper presented at the 30th Annual Meeting of the African Studies Association (ASA), Denver: Colorado (19–23 November 1987), p. 6.

8. "The N'Sele Manifesto of the *Mouvement Populaire de la Révolution*" (20 May 1967).

9. "Church and Authenticity in Zaïre, Special Note," *Pro Mundi Vita* 39: 2.

10. *Bureau de l'Enseignement National Catholique*, 1974.

11. "Church and Authenticity," 6. For further information on the subject, see Tharcisse Tshibangu, *Le propos d'une théologie africaine* (Kinshasa: Presses Universitaires du Zaïre, 1974).

12. Ibid.

13. Ibid.

14. Pablo Richard, "The Church of the Poor in the 1990s," *Challenge in Central America* 2:2 (Summer 1991): 11.

5

Ethnicity and Nationalism: Real Challenges to Multipartyism?

CONCEPTUALIZATION OF THE PROBLEM, OBJECTIVES, AND MAIN ARGUMENTS

The main objective of this chapter is to examine the role that ethnicity has played in African politics and its potentialities in the current democratic processes and in the search for a model of development. Some of the issues raised in this section have already been partially discussed in other chapters, specifically chapters 2 and 3. However, this chapter expands further on the question of whether ethnicity and nationalism can positively or negatively, or implicitly and explicitly, challenge the rise of multiparty democracy in Africa. The discussion is basically theoretical in content, but it also has a policy consideration. It critically examines the rise of ethnicity and nationalism as political claims and forces made by people and states to pursue their objectives. It identifies the general causes of this re-emergence and examines the dynamics of both ethnicity and nationalism in democratic discourses. Illustrations from many parts of Africa are included in the discussion to clarify the theoretical basis and assumptions.

The first part of this chapter is on the conceptualization of the *problématique* that is to say, the perception of the problem, the issues to be discussed, and the identification of the major arguments to be analyzed. The second part is an effort to define ethnicity and nationalism. The third part concerns their implications for the re-definition of democratic discourses in Africa.

Can the forces of ethnicity and nationalism impede the expansion and consolidation of democracy in Africa? Can they stop people from articulating human rights or self-determination issues? Is ethnicity philosophically antithetic to multipartyism in Africa? As Nnoli stated:

It has been argued that in Africa, democracy promotes subnational ethnic demands capable of pitting ethnic groups one against another in strifes that tear the country apart. This is because of the difficulty of an African opposition political party to justify its separate existence from the ruling party on the basis of some important and visible socioeconomic programmes.

Ethnicity provides one of the most convenient and appealing alternatives to such a programme. Political constituencies are often geographical in nature and quite often ethnically homogeneous. (1994, 10)

As convincing as the above statement may appear, it has to be critically understood within the general framework of the dynamics of the African state and of the national politic within the world political economy. One needs to be modest in examining the nature of ethnicity, nationalism, and democratic discourses in general terms because each African context has its own specificities and particularities in the way nationalism and democracy have been dealt with.

Democratic discourses, for instance, have taken different forms depending on the nature of state formation, the type of political culture and regime, the dynamics of civil society, and the relationship between the national and the global political economies. An understanding of the initial social, economic, and political conditions at the time when democratic movements occurred may help explain why ethnic and national forces have been behaving the way they do. Concerning the issue of caution related to the study of ethnicity, Osaghae stated:

The ethnic situation, involving the character of ethnic groups and the conflict among them, as well as their class, regional, racial, religious and other correlates and finally, the factors which make them politically salient, different from one society to another. For this reason, I have argued elsewhere, attempts to universalise the concept of ethnicity, for all their scientific merits, must be treated with great caution because they tend to gloss over the particularities which make ethnicity in the United States of America, for example, different from ethnicity in Africa. (1994, 1)

However, the underlying forces, or what Okwudiba Nnoli has called intervening variables[1] behind the rise of ethnicity, nationalism, and democracy, and the global context in which ethnicity, nationalism, and democracy have been functioning, produce relative similarities in terms of their general intended objectives. Despite difficulties in making generalizations, the approach at the historization of ethnicity and nationalism within the context of struggles toward democracy illuminates how the forces of the global system and its components—colonial and neo-colonial politics and policies, the market economy, transnational corporations and the national and international media—have given a generalized significance to ethnicity and nationalism. From this historization point of view, it becomes possible to show how ethnicity, nationalism, and democratic discourses have been heavily influenced by the dynamics of the world system. For instance, the choice of the colonial administrators and the Christian missionaries to locate themselves in a specific geographical space contributed to the process of the disorganization of ethnicity in that milieu. This choice supported the linking of the local economy and power with the dynamics of the global economy and world politics. This contemporary dynamics of the world, which is an important force of world politics, has been based on the claims of superiority of the so-called universal norms and culture.

The class analysis of the global economy, however, does not positively support the assumption of the success of universalism in Africa.

As Vicki Hesli stated: "Despite the fact that the achievement of political stability is to a large degree dependent upon the nature of the divisions within a society, many scholars, until recently, have neglected to systematically incorporate ethnicity into the study of political change."[2] As Osaghae noted: "In spite of the popularity of ethnic explanations in Africa, ethnicity remains heavily under-studied in several countries."[3] The tragic power struggles in Somalia, Burundi, and Rwanda, and the current experiences of the former Soviet Union and Eastern Europe, have reinforced the view that ethnicity and nationalism, especially their separatist aspects, are serious threats to stability in those regions. However, Hesli also indicates that: "If we accept the premise that ethnic identity is a natural basis for political organization and that nationalism as an ideology has proved its functional power through history, then any theory of democracy must incorporate contingencies for the resolution of ethnic conflict."[4]

Since the 1980s, with the rise of popular movements and various forms of struggles for liberal democracy, ethnicity and nationalism have re-emerged in African politics with a high degree of visibility. They are emerging after the nominal political independence of the African states has brought disillusionment to the majority of the African people. Many Africans, including intellectuals and politicians, have become much more ethnic than ever before in their discourses and their vision of how the national politics around them should be organized. What is the political and sociological significance of ethnicity and nationalism in the context of current multiparty democracies?

During the colonial period, the dominant paradigms in the social sciences, especially in anthropological and ethnological studies perceived ethnicity and nationalism as essentially destructive forces for modernization or Westernization. They were perceived to be essentially African pathologies. They were associated with negative particularism, parochialism, primordialism, and ahistorical thinking. In short, ethnicity, defined as "tribalism," was negatively perceived as a low sociological unit associated in a given social context. The so-called tribal people were defined as "pre-logical" and essentially static in their social organization. Ethnicity was also perceived as an exclusive social phenomenon within the destiny of the global capitalism and from the perspective of unilinear world history. Scholars such as E. David Apter, before becoming Africanist revisionists, representing conventional modernization theories with their universalistic perception of history and their anti-social movements' intellectual and political positions, defined ethnicity as an irrational phenomenon, a way of being that could not significantly contribute to global human emancipation. They believed that the market and liberal democracy with their rational choice and individualism can emancipate human beings and, in the case of Africa, rescue the entire society from collapsing. Although this perception of history is anti-scientific, it has influenced the general paradigms and policies articulated in the post-colonial era in Africa. For different reasons, the pan-Africanist perspective does not emphasize positive forces of identity based on ethnicity alone. It focuses on the common ideology and features.

The contemporary African state and country are essentially multi-ethnic and international. These two elements have, to a large extent, evolved in the processes of the state and societal building with the colonial and the post-colonial political societies. The effort to maintain an equilibrium between these dimensions by the colonial powers and later by the African nationalist elites, has not been peaceful in the areas of territorial boundaries in many regions as these boundaries were set up arbitrarily, at least from the point of view of the colonized (indiges), without paying much attention to their cultural and historical meaning. Thus, ethnic groups and sub-groups found themselves divided, located, and re-located between two or more territorial districts, provinces, or colonial states. This was almost a general rule in the colonies. Although the African political elites, for power and class economic interests, agreed to retain these boundaries and thus, voted in the Organization of African Unity (OAU) conference in Addis Ababa in 1963 for continuity and the status quo, many ethnic groups have consistently defied the functionality and legalism of these imposed boundaries.

The African state and society are also essentially heterogeneous with a few exceptions such as Somalia. Since the 1960s, there have been more than 70 territorial disputes in Africa, most of which had colonial origins and some of which resulted in violent actions.[5] Independence movements created opportunities for many ethnic groups to argue for unification and consequently for either secessionism or some form of relative political autonomy. This was the case, for instance, in the Pan-Ewe movement, the Federation of Bakongo, Tshombe's *Confédération des Association Tribales du Katanga* (CONAKAT), some Akan groups in the southern part of Côte d'Ivoire, and the current Tuareg movement in Mali and Niger. Thus, the dispute on geographical boundaries is still an unsolved political issue linked to ethnic nationalism and the state in African politics.

The practical adoption of multiparty democracy on a larger scale was attempted by the African political elites only at the end of the colonial era. Multiparty democracy has therefore been essentially a nationalistic and elitist phenomenon, although it emerged from within the framework of broad popular and social movements. As a nationalistic phenomenon, it takes the form of ethnic identity and affirmation. The recent cases of the collapse of the state and society in Liberia and Somalia, the massacres in Angola of Bakongo people and other Congolese in 1994, the mutual slaughter in Burundi and Rwanda between Hutus and Tutsis in 1994, the ethnic clashes in Lesotho between Basotho and other groups in 1991, the massacre and pillage in Lubumbashi (the Democratic Republic of Congo) of the people originally from the Kasaï provinces in 1993, and the ethnic struggles in Sierra-Leone, Malawi, and the Sudan, indicate that the associative and symbolic energies of this phenomenon cannot be denied in social science analysis.

Ethno-nationalism, known also as primary nationalism, has become one of the most visible forces in the current popular and social struggles toward democracy in Africa. It has re-emerged from different origins and philosophical bases. Liberal and multiparty democratic expressions in most parts of Africa have created space for the rise of strong ethnic and nationalistic sentiments. Generally, in Africa, the majority of people tend to perceive the struggles for democracy as inclusive or integrative processes within defined territorial boundaries.

However, since the 1970s and 1980s, especially at the end of the Cold War, the focus of scholarship on ethnicity and nationalism has taken different forms, depending on the school of thought. Interestingly, ethnicity (not tribe) began to be considered a relevant variable in the Eastern European social conflicts and dynamics. The claims of ethnicity are being linked once again with the reformist base that is rooted in demands for national autonomy and self-determination. In short, ethnicity and the violence that is associated with it have characterized the African power struggles in the search for democracy, and self-determination.

Whether ethnic-related violence has its roots in the de-construction or construction of the modern state or in the philosophy and policy of the distribution of resources within the world system, its impact on social progress raises many questions as to its relationship to the search for long lasting stability. Although ethnic violence is not new in the history of state formation, after the end of the Cold War, it has exploded nationally among oppressed or minority groups at a level that is unprecedented in the post-colonial period. Ethnic violence, though it may reflect specific concerns or particular conditions within a given context, should be understood in a broader context. It is partially the nature and character of the African state and the base of its legitimacy that are being seriously challenged by ethnic violence.

In the first and second chapters, multipartyism in Africa was defined as an effort by the state to accept peacefully or violently the establishment of a constitutional arrangement that allows two or more political parties to compete for public office (the presidency, seats in parliament and other positions at the local or regional level). Although the rules of competition have been somewhat defined in some cases, the notion of political competition has been obviously operating in a sociological environment that is different from that of the West. One may have the wrong impression that in Africa there is a permanent philosophical conflict between pluralistic political competition and the African metaphysics of collectiveness.

In discussing the challenges of ethnicity to democracy, some important questions must be posed to clarify the level of analysis. Have ethnicity and the violence that derives from some of its activities been challenging democratic institutions and political actors who aspire to be elected through democratic processes? Have they been challenging the political system at large? Is ethnic expression conflictual and violent by essence or in fact? Does ethnicity make Africa allergic to democracy? These questions may be difficult to clearly answer in this section because in Africa, the majority of people do not sharply separate political actors from the political institutions in which they function. That is to say, society has a monistic perception of the rules of political games and the makers of the rules. Therefore, it is historically correct to say that ethnic violence or other expressions that are positively or negatively related to it have been challenging both the existing political institutions and actors. What we have been observing in most cases in Africa reflects ethnic manipulation rather than ethnic conflict. What has been expected to be achieved through these challenges? Have they also challenged the dominant world ideologies embodied within the states?

One of the views articulated in this chapter is that, although ethnicity and nationalism do have their own internal dynamics (for instance, their own value systems, ethos, and cultural symbolisms), to understand them comprehensively, it is important to examine how they produce themselves locally and internationally. It is difficult to conceptualize ethnicity and nationalism as autonomous phenomena from the state formation and power consolidation in Africa. It is in relationship to the state and society that we can understand how they develop and function.

State formation is itself an international phenomenon. Ethnic and nationalistic forces were mobilized for the development and expansion of the African states. During the struggles for independence, with the support of ethnicity and nationalism, the African states organized coalitions either to act against the interests of foreign powers or to integrate them. (That is to say, to be part of the structures of the colonial political economy and the state.) In any case, as discussed later, the movements toward self-determination were essentially nationalistic and ethnic in their social appearance and linguistic expressions.

In the 1990s, with the massive challenges made by popular movements against states for many reasons, and the weakening of the African state in terms of its role in the international arena, manipulative ethnicity and petty bourgeois nationalism are playing new roles in African politics. Explicitly or implicitly, they are doing what the states should have been doing: that is, providing some security, no matter how fragile, to citizens at the time of the crisis of the global economy and considerable anarchic global competition.

Ethnicity and nationalism are not ontologically static concept; philosophically they cannot be perceived as agents of anti-democracy or anti-social progress. If given appropriate value systems or placed within a new political environment produced by popular revolution, societal consensus, or dialogical discourses, they can support and promote democratic discourses. In short, if ethnicity and nationalism are enlightened by the struggle for democratic ideals and values engendered by popular and social movements, they can become agents for social progress. However, the questions are: At what level, and under which conditions, can they become constructive forces for society at large? What kind of ethnicity and nationalism can be constructive or de-constructive for a given society? Some concrete illustrations will help shed light on the above questions and issues.

ETHNICITY AND NATIONALISM AS POLITICAL FORCES

Africa, the second largest continent, with an estimated 700 million people in 1995, constituting about 12 percent of the world population, is grouped into 54 independent countries (most of which were colonized by European states, with the exception of Liberia and Ethiopia, although they too became neo-colonial states) with more than 1,000 ethnic groups, each with its own particularities, traditions, and political space. There are also large socio-linguistic groupings and subgroupings in which many ethnic groups can be classified, for instance, the Akans, Arabs,

Bantus, Berbers, Hamites, Hausa, Malinke, Moors, Peuls, Pygmies, Tuaregs, Xhosa, Zulus, and Yoruba. There are many linguistic, social, and political similarities within these groupings. Nigeria, for instance, has between 250 and 400 ethnic groups. The Democratic Republic of Congo has more than 200 ethnic groups. Even small countries such as the Gambia with fewer than 1 million people has more than ten ethnic groups. Although so-called tribalism, as the creation of Western colonial scholarship and its political configurations, is perceived to be philosophically ahistorical, ethnicity can be a dynamic sociological and historical phenomenon.

Most people define themselves in terms of their geographical location, their language, their religion, and their local history, whether it is a glorious history or one of defeat. Ethnic affiliation is based on common economic, political, and socio-cultural characteristics. These characteristics are shaped by geography, a history of political struggle and metaphysical values (preservation of some basic moral values). As David Throup states:

Ethnic sub-nationalism has been as powerful a political force in most of Africa as territorial nationalism. In many parts of the continent ethnic sub-nationalist identity—tribalism—had developed before territorial identity. Indeed, based on a common culture, history, language and traditions, ethnic sub-nationalism in Africa appealed to those factors which had engendered European nationalism in the 19th century.[6]

People do not belong to ethnic groups and function within their structures simply as a matter of religious faith. The beliefs people have in ethnicity are a function of what it can offer. It is a historical and a sociological necessity. It plays the role of social and cultural security. What ethnicity may offer cannot be evaluated only in terms of material aspects, although those aspects are important. In the United States, for instance, in the most normal political circumstances, especially during the recent peaceful periods, people are proud to be identified with their past sociological origins, to be labeled Italian-American, Irish-American, Greek-American, or African-American, without necessarily expecting to have direct material gains from Italy, Ireland, Greece, or Africa. This was not the case at the turn of the century or during the era of the major wars when the single identification, "being American," was a unifying national force. The gains from ethnicity can be summarized as:

1. historical and cultural identification;
2. a sense of belonging to something larger;
3. and a sense of being functional and needed.

Thus, these gains can be used for promoting personal and national economic and political objectives on a long-term basis. This is not unique to Africa.

As already indicated, within the Western scholarships and policies, ethnicity in Africa has been perceived as the major factor that tends to impede the successful establishment of democracy and the promotion of development. This assertion has to be clarified in light of other pertinent arguments. The explanation of the violent manifestations associated with ethnicity in Africa can be found in non-ethnic discourses and structures. The level of distribution of political powers and social services, and the state of economic development, the nature of nationalistic political forces that were involved in the struggle for independence, the role of religion in the political process, the size of the country, and neighboring countries, and the policies of former colonial powers should also be taken into account in explaining why ethnicity behaves the way it does in post-colonial Africa. A critical examination of the relations between African states and the world economy, and how they deal with society, can provide an important analytical framework for understanding the nature of ethnicity within democratic processes.

In Africa, regardless of their ideological choices, states that have maintained a certain consistent minimum welfare policy or have had a relatively strong basis for welfare (for instance, in delivering system of the basic goods and services), and promoted a certain minimum dialogue with their citizens, and have kept a certain level of continuity of elite with the political alliances cut across ethnic cleavages, among other factors, those states have been likely, in some periods, to produce a relatively small chance of ethnic explosion incidences. Côte d'Ivoire, Gabon, and the Gambia, until recently, are some examples. Thus, the dysfunctionality of the state, that is to say, its inability to aggregate, make compromises, or satisfy promised social interests, constitutes one of the most important factors that have caused the re-emergence of new configurations of ethnicity and nationalism. That is to say, the level of ethnic violence can be measured by the intensity of the state's alienation from the society and people at large, and the relative openness of the process of political formation. In short, the character of a given African state and the nature of its economy will likely determine the role of ethnicity in politics in that national milieu. Negativity related to ethnicity is partially due to the nature of the intervention of the state in the re-mapping of ethnic groups and to the history of inter-ethnic relations in a given social context (Osaghae, 1994). Countries such as Nigeria, Kenya, and the Democratic Republic of Congo, which have strongly intervened in the management of ethnicity, have produced stronger negative responses from ethnic groups than those where the state's intervention was relatively smoother and inter-ethnic relations have been relatively more peaceful (for example, Botswana, the Gambia, and Mauritius).

There are those who argue that ungovernability or governability of the state in developing world is also due to its size and population mix, examples, Nigeria, the Sudan, and the Democratic Republic of Congo. However, Togo, Sierra Leone, and Liberia, for instance, are among the smallest countries in Africa, and yet they too have produced their share of ethnic violence and social tragedies. The ungovernability of Nigeria or the Sudan, for example, is not a function of their size. It is a complex phenomenon. However, ungovernability can also be partially explained in terms of how a given state was born, how the processes of dislocation or re-location of new and old political and social interests were established, the nature of internal dynamics within ethnic groups, and the structure of the societies and how they evolved over time. What is nationalism, and how has it manifested itself in various parts of Africa?

Although Africa is the only region among developing regions of the world system where there is no consistent and common functioning global nationalist movement (common societal project), African conditions, social and political systems, and internal contradictions have produced different forms of local nationalism. Despite the controversial role that various forms of nationalism have been playing in modern politics and this role's policy implications, nationalism has been one of the dominant social and political forces in contemporary Africa. It is difficult to re-examine the structures, policies, and ideologies of political independence and neo-colonial politics without referring to it.

Nationalism is a political response to, or reaction from, colonial political mapping. An important topic is the kind of political community and political human beings nationalists have envisioned in their societal projects. What kind of nationalism are we talking about, and what is the nature of the policy development agenda they have engendered, if any? An analysis based on a policy agenda requires a combination of theoretical generalizations along with some specific examples.

Nationalism has generally been defined in the Western literature as the emotional feeling of belonging to a cohesive social group wherein people share common characteristics: linguistic, political, religious, and geographical. These characteristics are functional; they create and impose a consensus on the goals and purposes of a given political community. National consciousness seems to be even more of a subjective phenomenon than class consciousness. It is a system of beliefs that puts a certain group of people together. It is an ideology. Ernest Gellner defines it in these terms:

Nationalism is primarily a political principle, which holds that the political and the national unit should be congruent. Nationalism as a sentiment, or as a movement, can best be defined in terms of this principle. Nationalist sentiment is the feeling of anger aroused by the violation of the principle, or the feeling of satisfaction aroused by its fulfillment. A nationalist movement is actuated by a sentiment of this king.[7]

Although nationalism in which people fight to preserve their values and identities is not new in contemporary African politics and history, the modern versions of nationalism have some unique characteristics that are related to its origins. It is, for one thing, a product of the colonial and imperialist invasions, and it is strongly associated with slavery, colonialism, neo-colonialism, and many other forms of imperialism and domination. In this sense, African nationalism in the contemporary and post-colonial periods did not emerge as a normal or natural internal evolutionary process of history, or as a result of the maturity of the African traditional and local political systems. That is to say that internal contradictions in the social systems or power struggle within a given class, did not produce contemporary nationalism. Contemporary African nationalism is different from the type of nationalism expressed among the Ashanti, for instance, prior to their incorporation into the British colonial unit of the Gold Coast and the larger colonial empire. Rather, it is a product of the contradictions of colonial and neo-colonial politics and policies. Thus, from the point of view of the colonial political economy, it is not necessarily a cultural and psychological expression of certain ethnic groups; rather, it is a political expression that uses a cultural language. In colonial Africa, the rise of nationalism is associated with feelings of inadequacy, dislocation, and dysfunctionality.

Different forms of nationalism in Africa have used different voices in various ethnic groups, classes, and cultural associations for a variety of objectives. That is to say, nationalism has manifested itself in many different forms, including religious, political, and artistic. Whether it is the expression of the Ewe elite in Ghana and Togo in the 1960s against the British and French imperialistic policies respectively, or a separatist political statement of Ojuku in Nigeria (the Biafra war and Igbo nationalism in Eastern Nigeria) at the end of the 1960s, Tshombe's claims for secessionism in Katanga in the 1960s (in the Democratic Republic of Congo), Garang's national liberation struggle in the Sudan since the 1980s, or the Eritrean or Tigrean separatist struggles against the Ethiopian government in the 1970s, 1980s and early 1990s, nationalism has challenged the existing structures of power with the message that nationalists tend to see themselves politically as being better than others and that they can make a difference. Of course, the challenge of integrationism or assimilationism is different from the challenge of separatism or independence. In all cases, however, regardless of its nature and history, nationalism embodies ideas and ideals in a search for newness, an illusion of newness, or a hope to create newness. Its actualization depends principally on a given historical and political context.

As documented elsewhere,[8] several sorts of nationalism have been engendered in the 20th century in Africa: those promoted by the colonial states (reformist or eclectical conservative nationalism), those associated essentially with local social and cultural conditions (separatist nationalism), and those located mainly in the structures of the international economic, social, and political conditions of oppressed groups or communities (radical leftist nationalism). This categorization can be challenged, in that small and spontaneous movements may not fit into its logic.

All three of these categories have operated in the same broad political space, sometimes simultaneously. Political forces involved in each category, and their social and political relations with the dominant political system, make a big difference in the way each has perceived its role in the local environment and the international context. Historically all have been affected differently by the policies of the state and the forces of the international political economy. Each has reacted differently to the oppressive political structures imposed on a given social milieu, and most of them have advocated some kind of decolonization, although with different agendas, hopes, and actors. Though it is difficult to generalize the above categorizations, they provide a basis for analysis.

Reforms that originated with the colonial states, whether British or French, started in the years after World War II as a result of the impact of the war on colonial politics, power struggles in the metropolitan countries, and the emergence of local social movements. Colonial powers started to reorganize local politics for their self-interest rather than to help the people. They decided to minimize their exploitative policies and make their politics and policies more acceptable to Africans (though not necessarily to the majority of Africans). In the former French colonies, for instance, the abolition of forced labor by *Loi* Félix Houphouët-Boigny on April

11, 1946, and the passing of *Loi-Cadre* on June 23, 1956, promoted the reformist policies that led to autonomy, and then independence. The leaders of those nationalist movements were the emerging African petty bourgeoisie, who aspired to replace the colonial ruling classes by collaborating with them.

With a few exceptions, such as Modibo Kéita, Julius Nyerere, and Ahmed Sékou Touré, most of the African petty bourgeois leaders believed in the cult of liberal democracy, as brilliantly discussed by Chinweizu in *The West and the Rest of Us*. Liberal constitutions were intended to protect individuals' rights to vote and participate in national politics through political organizations. Parliamentary democracy was adopted in most parts of Africa. Usually, however, soon after independence, liberal democracy became dysfunctional. In the case of the Congo, for example, it functioned less than two months. The reasons for its failures are numerous and quite controversial and include the following:

- Democracy was hijacked by small African elite.
- It became too bureaucratic and artificially procedural, and it was too expensive for the ordinary people.
- Its conceptualization was alien to many local practices.
- An external factor intervened that did not allow the democratic process to properly function and mature.
- Above all, it did not take into account the collective and humanistic nature of the African way of life.
- In short, nationalists did not push for transformative relations or structural changes within their own political parties.

At the economic level, *les nationalistes d'État* ("the nationalists of the state") also maintained *laissez-faire* economic principles or capitalism, and they deliberately chose to continue close economic ties with the former colonial masters. Leaders like the late Félix Houphouët-Boigny, Léopold Sedar Senghor, and the late Jomo Kenyatta could not envision working without strong cooperation with their former colonial masters, though it should be noted that, in some cases, economic nationalism was tried. They intended to Africanize capitalism. As Fanon stated:

The objective of the nationalist parties from a certain given period is, as we have seen, strictly national. They mobilize the people with slogans of independence, and for the rest leave it to future events. When such parties are questioned on the economic program of the state that they are clamoring for, or on the nature of the regime which they propose to install, they are incapable of replying, because, precisely, they are completely ignorant of their own economy. (1991, 150)

Another characteristic of this nationalism is the perception of political independence. Political independence was viewed as a *sine qua non* for political change. Ben-Bella of Algeria, Kenyatta of Kenya, Lumumba of the Congo, Nasser of Egypt, Nkrumah of Ghana, Nyerere of Tanzania, and Sékou Touré of Guinea-Conakry all believed that the struggle for independence and self-determination, regardless of the form it took for solving African problems, including new political alliances and Africa's involvement in international affairs, needed to be addressed first. Once one becomes politically independent, then one can pursue other agendas. The problem with this reasoning is that independence is not the equivalent of the people's sovereignty. Although the people's support was crucial in the movement toward decolonization, state sovereignty was separated both from the people and from societal sovereignty.

The significance of political independence is a matter of policy choice issue. Thus, it is a debatable issue. However, generally one can discuss political independence in terms of the relations between domestic and international policies and their implications for the performance of local politics and economy. This significance is not a matter of faith or a religious doctrine, for people are generally pragmatic in their way of measuring or evaluating change vis-à-vis their social environment and their living standard. In this regard, the meaning of political independence depends on the performance of the state in tackling the enormous social and economic problems inherited from the colonial administration. Though the issue of the nature of independence is important, the nationalist-reformists believed that nationalism is de facto an instrument for acquiring state power. Does this kind of nationalism have anything in common theoretically with the separatist nationalism that has also developed in Africa?

This separatist nationalism generally starts spontaneously on the local cultures' premises or histories; that is to say, on narrow or limited agenda related to the immediate needs. Though some movements gradually develop relatively clear political objectives later, their immediate objectives are not mainly political, if one defines politics, within the framework of social and national movements, as a process or activity of acquiring state or community power. They do, however, have a clear picture of who the enemy is. The Mau-Mau in Kenya, the Maji-Maji in Tanganyika, Mahdism in the Sudan, Kimbanguism or Kitawalism or the Simba or the Mai-Mai in the Congo, all mainly resisted the undemocratic, militaristic, racist, and exploitative nature of colonial politics. With the exception of a few movements like Mahdism, most forms of this kind of nationalism did not seem to produce consistent institutionalized ideologies and politics that could seriously challenge capitalism, Eurocentrism, and Christianity in a broader context.

One of the major tendencies of separatist nationalism is its advocacy of some kind or syncretism at best. Though Kimbanguism, for instance, uses the Bible as a holy book of reference, and it has a separatist concept of a new world order and ethos, it does not preach integration into Western Christianity and its values. Kimbangu is an African prophet. His missionaries are not Belgians, Americans, or British: they are Africans. Mahdism, for example, has been considered as a jihad, a religious war. It was founded on Islamic doctrines and laws. As a popular social phenomenon, it was based on anti-colonial politics and religion, for ideologically, there could be no compromise between Mahdism and British imperialism in the Sudan.

The political dimensions of this nationalism cannot be underestimated. However, it does not provide a clear picture of political objectives and the kinds of political systems to establish in Africa, or what role Africa should be playing in the international political economy.

Radical leftist nationalism has been influenced by either Marxism-Leninism, Maoism, or contemporaryAfrican political thought. What has been referred to, ideologically, as an Afro-Marxism or African-Marxism is characterized by its use of class struggle as a social theory of change. Afro-socialism, especially Nyerere's dominant variant, is characterized as a home-grown socialism in that it has denied the existence of class conflicts in African social formations. For Afro-Marxists such as Amilcar Cabral, Kwame Nkrumah, and Samora Machel, revolutionary nationalism is a product of class antagonisms in a given society, and those antagonisms are historically rooted in the structures of the colonial political economy. It is the exploitation and unequal distribution of wealth produced in Africa with African cheap labor and resources, and the colonial control over the ownership of the means of production and surplus labor, that led to massive social revolts and strikes aimed at leading to a more organized movement.

From the perspectives of some dominant segments within radical leftist nationalism, political independence has to be obtained either by popular struggles, armed struggles, or a combination of both. The nature of the armed struggle varies from country to country, or from one movement to another, but the main belief is that armed struggle may contribute to a more rapid increase in national consciousness and commitment for change than the gradualism and accommodationism that has been opted for by the conservative nationalists. The tragedy of the war is itself viewed as a force for change because revolutionary warriors attempt to tackle the problems produced out of the social contradictions in a given social system.

Whether one agrees or disagrees with the above reasoning, what is important is that, generally, radical leftist nationalists seem to have been more political and combative in their attitudes than other types of nationalists. They have had a sense of history and have defined the enemies of their societies more sharply than accommodationists. They had some visions or ideals of the type of society to be built, and their leaders tended to be prophetic in their politics and deterministic in their policies. The history of society is defined as a permanent history of struggle. In national liberation movements such as those that occurred in Algeria, Angola, Guinea-Bissau, Mozambique, Namibia, and Zimbabwe, political independence has been defined as a radical change in power relations both within the state and outside the country.

Some radical nationalists, such as Gaddafi of Libya, Mengistu (the former leader of Ethiopia), the late Sankara of Burkina Faso, and even Rawlings of Ghana (before he gave up an attempt at radical central planning and adopted realistic options), have come to power through military coups. Later they tried to transform their political organizations into social or popular movements. Some African leaders and masses, however, did not opt for armed struggles to obtain their nominal political independence, although they adopted some radical policies in their state.

The late Modibo Kéita in Mali initiated, in the 1960s, socialist and pan-Africanist programs. The late Sékou Touré of Guinea-Conakry, after voting "no" to the 1958 referendum proposed by the French government with the cooperation of the African elites, as a member of a trade union mobilized the workers and the emerging middle class through a radical nationalism that combined elements of African socialism, pan-Africanism, and scientific socialism. Although Sékou Touré's nationalism became "fetishized" later, ideologically it was too far left as compared to other types of nationalism. In the former People's Republic of Congo (Congo-Brazzaville), scientific socialism was adopted in 1963 and Marxism-Leninism in 1968. As well described by Ernest Wamba-dia-Wamba, radicalism in the Congo was trapped by the contradictions of the society and state: power struggles, state repressive strategies, lack of implementation of real economic programs, and conflicts of interests between the petty bourgeois Marxists and the masses of people (1987, 96–110).

In Ethiopia, Marxist-Leninist ideology was officially proclaimed the ideology of the state and party in 1985, and the working class theoretically became the vanguard class with strong support from the ideologues. The end of the Marxist-Leninist regime of Mengistu indicates that, at least in part, the regime did not learn much from the mistakes that the Eastern European states were trapped in for many years. The conflicts between ideologues, working class citizens (cadres), and peasants increased quickly as many members of the society were alienated from the actions and policies of the state. Whether or not the Ethiopian radical leftist ideology succeeded in being incorporated into public policies, what is more important is how Africa at large, as a political entity, has been perceived by this kind of progressive nationalism.

Perception is also a matter of how effectively national policies articulate African problems. How did radical leftist nationalism deal with the issues of the performance (or lack of it) of the African states, with their policies and their role in international relations? To shed some light on this subject, a brief discussion of the political philosophy of Burkina Faso under the late Sankara may be helpful.

Burkina Faso is interesting because the state, and not the masses of people or proletariat, created a revolutionary dictum.[9] Of course, there were dynamic relations between various social forces and the state, but there is no historical or policy evidence that indicates that Sankara, who emerged as a leader produced by popular struggle, was acting mainly in the name of a given social class, such as the proletariat (or was representing primarily a fixed ideology or interests of such a social class), although he has been strongly influenced by the working class theory of social change. He advocated the transformation the state apparatus, and he mobilized people, especially youth, to advance and support this revolution. Sankara and his team believed that the state should be an educator and an organizer. It was conceived of as an enlightened social force.

Sankara and the commandos of the unit from Pô came to power by a military coup d'état after Upper Volta, now Burkina Faso, went through a political crisis (that is, a power struggle) similar in nature, but not in intensity, to the one that crippled Uganda after Idi Amin. It should be mentioned that at the beginning the new military officers who captured the state power did not have a strong political base in Ouagadougou, the capital city. From Maurice Yaméogo, who was the first president of the Upper Volta, a member of the *Rassemblement Démocratique*

Africain (RDA), and a petty bourgeois, who strongly supported the idea of cooperation with France, to the emergence of the military coups of Lamizana and Zerbo, the fragile legitimacy of the state created a general political crisis. Among other effects, the power struggle created political instability and ethnic violence among various social forces.

Sankara was brought into the government of Major Jean Baptiste Ouédraogo in November 1982, as prime minister. Two ideological tendencies characterize this government of the Council for the People's Salvation (CSP). First, there were those who believed in the so-called traditional or professional role of the military. Their claim was that their role was to bring and maintain order and promote peace. They had a technical view of the world. Second, there were those who believed that soldiers should get involved in politics, just like any other citizens; but they must transform themselves into real social forces by becoming dynamic human beings promoting social progress. Sankara was the leading force in this category. The transformation of the state, especially the military apparatus, is particularly interesting in an analysis of new political remapping. Sankara was convinced that, without such a transformation, his political agenda was not going to advance well. His objective was not to dismantle the state, but to try to transform it and make it more socially dynamic. The role of a soldier, in this thinking, is twofold: educator and builder. Thus, he decided to challenge the existing structures of power because they were based on a neo-colonial political philosophy and social arrangements and were also restricted mainly to serving state elites and capitalists.

Sankara's objective was, first of all, to democratize the army; he believed that democracy had to start with the army because soldiers have the role of protecting people. In this view, those who protect people must be democrats and not dictators, not enemies of the people. In fact, CSP was born as a result of this claim. Democratizing meant creating mechanisms through which each military unit would be represented in the general military assembly of the CSP. Clearly, this would change the apolitical character of the colonial and neo-colonial army in Burkina Faso, and this democratization would eventually create a people's army. It is only then that soldiers could start becoming educators and builders.

In the center of Sankara's theory of political change is the concept of democracy. Indeed, the most important feature of the CSP was its search for democracy. For Sankara, it was impossible to fight poverty and social injustice without acquiring the people's full participation from all segments of Burkinabè society. He pursued a revolutionary democracy to combat underdevelopment. As Guy Martin said:

The primary objective of the revolution is to take power out of the hands of a national bourgeoisie and their imperialist allies and put it in the hands of people. As the only legal and legitimate repository of political power, the people should be invested with this power [by which] they are to assume their responsibilities and to control their destiny. (1989, 63)

The CSP set up people's revolutionary courts that would be more accessible to all. It intended to get rid of bourgeois laws—the laws of the rich—that were considered important contradictions in a society where 95 percent of the people were illiterate and poor. Thus, they decided to establish a court system that would be more accessible and less costly to all. Sankara said, concerning the reasons for forming the new courts: "Comrades, the People's Revolutionary Courts are sounding the death knell of Roman law; they are playing the swan song of the alien Napoleonic social law that has marginalized so very many of our people while declaring sacred the illegitimate and unjust privileges of the minority class" (Anderson, 1988, 61).

This theory of democratic politics was expanded to include other key issues, such as women's emancipation, African culture, and land reform, but it was far from covering all aspects or sectors of the society. The resistance was strong from various segments of society, including some groups of intellectuals (especially those who had special power linkages with France), traditional political elite that owned land, and top bureaucrats in the public service who had properties. In addition, time constraints were an important factor in the implementation of a given policy. Sankara and his associates wanted to accomplish much of their revolutionary task in a short period of time, without sufficiently preparing and educating people about the new situation and its individual and collective social and economic impact. The notion of urgency did not have a strong local political base.

In addition to popular democracy, which was the essence of Sankara's theory of social change, his position on Africa's international relations was ideologically radical. He thought that Africa must count on itself first, that is to say on its own human and material resources, culture, and power. Sankara revived pan-Africanism, and he did so at a time when most African states had started to participate in the Structural Adjustment Programs (SAPs) of the World Bank and stabilization programs of the IMF. As indicated earlier, the concept of global African nationalism and ideology threatened most African states and ruling classes and the Western powers. The opposition to it was massive, well organized, and predictable, even among some heads of state in the West African region. For Sankara, this concept has to transform an African state; that is to say, its role, its structure, and its objectives must be changed to fulfill pan-Africanist aims. The structure of the existing African state and power relations are the impediments for the actualization of pan-Africanism. Though Sankara did not advocate the death of the African state, he believed that pan-Africanism could contribute to its transformation, and he based his argument on culture and ideology. Ethnicity was not perceived as a dividing force except if used by the representatives of the imperialist powers for their own interests. Ethnic cultural diversity was the thread of African common cultural foundations. According to Sankara, Africa has only one color, and it is one of African unity. As he said:

Our ancestors in Africa were involved in their form of development. We do not want these great African sages to be written out of history. This is why we have created a center for the search of the black man in Burkina Faso. At this center we will study the origins of the black man, the evolution of his culture and his music around the world, as well as his dress, his cuisine, his languages the world over. In short, we will study everything that can enable us to affirm our own identity. (Anderson, 1988, 75)

The formation of pan-Africanism is thus based on the sense of a common culture. It is the choice of a new ideology strongly rooted in popular democracy. To advance his new ideas and policy, Sankara's first effort was to mobilize people, especially youth and women. The second effort he undertook was to educate and organize different social groups, and the third was to try to implement his ideas into policies. However, Sankara did not finish his job, for he was brutally assassinated in a bloody military coup d'état, which resulted from a power struggle orchestrated by his best friend and comrade, Blaise Compaoré, who took over state power.

The problems and contradictions of radical leftist nationalism cannot be analyzed and understood in isolation from the broader political situation.

IMPLICATIONS OF ETHNICITY AND NATIONALISM FOR STRUGGLES FOR DEMOCRACY

The major goal of ethnicity and nationalism has been self-determination. Ethnic sentiments and nationalistic forces or organizations have questioned some of the practices and policies of contemporary states. Most of these states, for various reasons, especially for power consolidation and strategic purposes, created in the past some room for some ethnic groups, or social categories within ethnic groups, to partially participate in the political process in their countries. Ethnic groups that have been functionally or ideologically associated with state powers have also benefited more than those with no such association. As David Throup stated: "The statist nature of African economies is partly a survival from the colonial era, but government intervention, as noted above, is also a product of the clientist nature of African politics, where supporters are rewarded and potential rivals bought off by a share of rewards from the state-controlled pork barrel."[10]

Examples of Tutsis in Burundi and Hutus in Rwanda are cases in point. The Tutsis perceive themselves as superior because they were chosen by the Belgian colonial power to play a special role of intermediary political forces in the colonization process. When it comes to power control, the Tutsis, who were in the center of the state power, at large defined the After-the independence to be equal to before-independence, the situation which the Hutus did not accept. The economic, political, and social conditions and the population pressure in relation to resources have been produced by this power relation has led to numerous genocides in both sides.

However, not all African politicians in the post-colonial era have, always, used ethnicity or cultural regional affinity, regardless of national political circumstances, as the only instrument of power consolidation. For example in Zaïre, although Mobutu's politics have had strongly ethnic support, the region of *Equateur* (Bandaka) where Mobutu came from, with the exception of his own village of Gbadolite, is not better off in terms of infrastructures than other regions that Mobutu consciously neglected. The late Félix Houphouët-Boigny of Côte d'Ivoire did not give privileges to the region of *Baoulé*[11] in terms of the distribution of power and resources, with the exception of his own village, Yamoussoukro. He ruled Côte d'Ivoire on the Akan (*Baoulé*) political philosophy but not with a *Baoulé* elite. And the *Parti Démocratique de Côte d'Ivoire* (PDCI) was not a *Baoulé*-based party.

The ethnic questioning, whether it is in the form of power struggle, like in Côte d'Ivoire and Kenya, or in the form of separatist arguments, like in Chad and Sudan, has created its own dynamism and social ramifications; that is to say, its own traditions. It is clear that if the Western imperialist powers and their dominant institutions do not intervene directly in Africa to maintain the status quo or stop the process of transformation of liberal democratic movements into social democracy, ethnicity and nationalism may force the African state to redefine itself. From the point of view of ethnicity, this redefinition can become more pragmatic than normative. This is so because the major problem of Africa today, as perceived by many Africans and reflected in current African conditions, is not only the lack of democracy, although this has been one of the major factors that impeded development, but the expanding poverty, and the alienation of most of the people in many ethnic groups from the means of production and state power.

Rivalry (or competition) among ethnic groups is a real social phenomenon in most parts of Africa. However, as stated by Osaghae, ethnic tensions are not inevitable. Rivalry is due, to a large extent, to the fact that national economic resources are scarce and access to them takes the form of power struggle.[12] Within the framework of the lack of democracy, the groups that have been in power have not felt compelled to share resources with other ethnic groups. Will resources be distributed equally through new policies if current democratic movements succeed in establishing democracy? One of the characteristics of democratic discourses is that people must know what their rights are. The process of identifying rights and using them for people's emancipation will require the institutionalization of popular education in many parts of the continent.

To adequately deal with poverty, the African state and people will have to be more imaginative and pragmatic. From the nationalistic point of view, the redefinition of the African state should be more ideological than pragmatic. The argument has been that the struggle for democracy should be dealing with the question of what kind of society ought to be built. The nationalistic arguments may promote democracy with the conviction that the new democratic society ought to be structurally different from the neo-colonial society. Thus, their arguments are strongly related to those of social and economic development.

The movements for power consolidation have used ethnicity and nationalism in Africa because these two forces can be easily manipulated. The recent ethnic conflicts that have emerged in most parts of the continent have a tone of political struggle: for instance, those in Cameroon, the Democratic Republic of Congo, Congo-Brazzaville, Côte d'Ivoire, Kenya, Liberia, Nigeria, Somalia, and the Sudan. Many ethnic conflicts in Africa are not ontologically ethnic. Those conflicts are not caused because ethnic groups want to assert their superiority. Rather, the petty bourgeois struggles for capturing state power, or maintaining the status quo that have created conditions for ethnic conflicts to arise. In Liberia, for instance, since the assassination of President Samuel Kanyon Doe in September 1990 by Prince Johnson through the power struggle initially led by Charles Taylor (elected president in the June 1997 presidential election), ethnic configurations have been influential. The Krahn group, which was linked to Doe by the fact that he was Krahn, and the Mandingo group, whose elite shared power with Doe, were considered by many other ethnic groups to be the enemies of Liberia and democracy. Although the situation of new alliances between ethnicity and political parties has somewhat been produced among the major fighting groups in Liberia, the ethnic element of this struggle is still central.

Political nationalism articulates possibilities for self-determination, political autonomy, and cultural identity. These elements are vital for the success of democratic principles and policies. Although the current democratic movements in Africa tend to focus on the universalism of protective rights, and freedom of an individual and of religion, some nationalistic political tendencies reflect an effort to de-link from the universalism of the world system, for instance, Islamic fundamentalism in Algeria, Egypt, and the Sudan. Through democratic movements, many sub-regions have been fighting to acquire some autonomy, like the *Casamançais* movement in Senegal. In the Democratic Republic of Congo, federalism has re-emerged as an alternative to the existing (Mobutuist) unitary system of the state. Among some Nigerian intellectuals, secessionist thought is being revisited in their political discourses. In short, ethnicity and nationalism may contribute to making the democratic discourses in Africa more real in terms of the basis of their cultural symbolisms, more pragmatic in terms of dealing with the direct local social issues, especially if they are articulated with a considerable dose of a consistent ideology and a national consciousness based on the concept of "we versus they" and "us versus them." "We are not French, American, or German." "We are Algerian, Ivorian, Ghanaian, Malian, Nigerian, South African, and Congolese." The problem is that "we versus they" is also used locally or nationally. This may lead to rethink the possibility of creating new societies different from past ones if power and social relations are changed through some form of collective struggle and collective vision of society. The new society cannot be envisioned if the existing democratic discourses do not seriously address the vital question of poverty as it relates to the issues of distribution of power and resources, protection of individual and social rights, and political participation. If the current democratic discourses do not restore the notion of social adequacy that ethnicity, as a collective entity, lost, African societies may plunge into nationalistic predicaments with the sense of no hope and no future. Ethnicity and nationalism can be emancipated in Africa if the liberal democracy of the petty bourgeoisie that is centered on individual rights and elections is transformed into social democracy as a result of the people's struggles against social injustice and poverty. As Nnoli states:

Although in reality ethnic factions of the ruling class seek only advantages for themselves in competition with one another, they usually couch their ethnic demands in terms of justice and equality. But democracy recognizes the equal rights of all ethnic groups, and fights against the privileged and nepotism of the advantaged and disadvantaged groups alike. It seeks to appraise each concrete ethnic question from the point of view of removing all inequality, all privileges and all exclusiveness. It emphasizes equal opportunities for all groups to a share of national life both in production and distribution. (1994, 48)

This national life has yet to be redefined in many parts of Africa. Democracy cannot positively progress within the framework of parochial nationalism as developed in the past in many African countries. The industrial countries with their functional liberal democracies have been highly nationalistic and patriotic. This is the case, for instance, in the United States, France, Japan, and Germany. The most pressing issues in African politics and political economy should be how to advance a form of functioning democracy without alienating any citizen and deal consciously with poverty as the number-one enemy of the African people.

NOTES

1. Okwudiba Nnoli, *Ethnicity and Democracy in Africa: Intervening Variables*, CASS Occasional Monograph no. 4 (Oxford: Malthouse, 1994).

2. Vicki L. Hesli, "Political Institutions and Democratic Governance in Divided Societies" in *Democratic Theory and Post-Communist Change*, ed. Robert D. Grey (Upper Saddle River, NJ: Prentice Hall, 1997), p. 202.

3. Eghosa Osaghae, *Ethnicity and Its Management in Africa: The Democratization Link*, CASS Occasional Monograph no. 2 (Oxford: Malthouse, 1994).

4. Hesli, "Political Institutions."

5. Most parts of the discussion on nationalism have been articulated in the author's book *Political Re-mapping of Africa* (Lanham, MD: University Press of America, 1994).

6. David Throup, "The Colonial Legacy," in *Conflict in Africa*, ed. Oliver Furley (London: I.B. Tauris Publishers 1995), p. 245.

7. Ernest Gellner, "Nations and Nationalism," in *Conflict After the Cold War: Arguments on Causes of War and Peace*, ed. Richard K. Betts (New York: Macmillan, 1994), p. 280.

8. See Lumumba-Kasongo, *Political Re-mapping*.

9. This case has been analyzed in depth in another book by the author entitled *Nationalistic Ideologies, Their Policy Implications in African Politics* (Lewiston, NY: Edwin Mellen Press, 1991).

10. Throup, " The Colonial Legacy," p. 261.

11. The late Félix Houphouët-Boigny was born in the family of a *Baoulé* chief. At the age of five, he inherited the chieftaincy, although he did not actually exercise power until later. *Baoulé* is an Akan group and is the largest ethnic group in Côte d'Ivoire.

12. See for instance, the case of Liberia.

6

The Military Factor in
the Current Democracy Equation

INTRODUCTION: OBJECTIVES AND ISSUES

The main objectives in this chapter are to examine the role of the military in current African democratic movements and to discuss the relationship between military dogmatisms and the people's demands for advancing democratic discourses. The chapter also briefly discusses the historical background of the rise of military regimes or armies as ruling elites in Africa. Although the observations are intended to be general and theoretical, the chapter will briefly discuss some of the specific characteristics of military regimes in Africa and the reasons why soldiers claim to and do capture state power.

The military intervention in African politics prior to the end of the Cold War era has been extensively studied; and an important body of literature has been produced by well-known scholars of militarism, such as Julius Ihonvbere (1991 and 1986), Samuel Decalo (1978), W. F. Gutteridge (1975), Claude Welch (1970), Henry Bienen (1968), Morris Janowitz (1964), and John Johnson (1962). Although with a certain level of skepticism, this intervention was previously perceived by modernization theorists such as E. David Apter and Samuel Huntington as a stabilizing political force or a modernizing phenomenon in Africa. However, social and economic facts show that the level of underdevelopment in most African countries and social class and ethnic tensions have gradually intensified during the military regimes, making the modernizing and stabilizing arguments and their assumptions problematic.

The end of the Cold War between the West and East, the re-emergence of popular and democratic movements in the former Eastern Europe and in the South, and the restoration of multipartyism globally have led scholars to re-visit the study of militarism. The violent military coup d'état in Congo-Brazzaville made by Sassou Nguesso's cobra forces in which General Nguesso recaptured power in October 1997 and another military coup d'état led by Johny Koroma, a low-level military officer, on May 25, 1997 in Sierra Leone, which overthrew the elected government headed by President Ahmed Tejan Kabbah, is a reminder that militarism cannot be counted out yet in African politics despite the demand and claims for democracy. Kabbah was elected president in February 1996. With the military assistance of the Ecomog led by Nigeria, Kabbah has been re-stated as the president of Sierra Leone in early 1998.

The working hypothesis in this chapter is that if democracy movements and multipartyism succeed in positively transforming the African state and power relations between state apparatuses, the character of the elite, the economy, and society, people in uniforms may go back to their barracks and play their conventional role of the guardians of the state and society. However, if local and international conditions, as reflected in the national configurations of power and the economy that have produced militarism in the past do not qualitatively change through the dynamics of multiparty democracy, there are likely to be more military coup d'états in the 21st century in Africa. Furthermore, if the social and technical conditions in the armed forces continue to be degraded by the economic conditionalities and the crisis of the Structural Adjustment Programs (SAPs) of the World Bank, the likelihood for the soldiers to protest is high. Their protest mechanisms are different from other social classes protests because they control the means of coercion: guns. An important question is: If the military regimes return with full energies and take the control over state power, as is likely to be the case within the existing level of poverty or underdevelopment in Africa, how will they respond effectively to the challenges of global economic competition, the demand from internal forces and external powers for economic reforms, the rise of ethnic nationalism, and the social tensions among the African *nouveaux riches*?

A combination of elements of history and theories of the state will guide the arguments and conclusion of this chapter. The discussion of the role of military forces in a democracy or in a transition toward a democracy is also a matter of understanding the political history of a given country, especially as related to state formation and the nature of forces such a history has produced through different generations of the African people.

The general image of the African state and society in the 1970s and 1980s was one of dictatorship, natural disaster, famine, poverty, and disconnection between the state and society. However, as a result of the contradictions of these phenomena, there are also people who have been struggling to liberate themselves from their oppressive conditions. Popular movements rose up in the late 1980s and the early 1990s, within the context of militarism and deteriorating economic conditions. Within the parameters of current democracy movements and the efforts of popular movements to challenge the African military and civilian autocrats to establish some form of democracy and promotion of economic rights, an analysis of how the military factor is perceived and how it is understood is vital and challenging. In relationship to the global economy, militarism is a dependent variable. The military factor, as either a political risk factor from the point of view of investors, or a power struggle from the point of view of the national elite, has only indirectly been an issue for grassroots movements' debates and actions because by nature this factor is an elitist and hierarchical phenomenon and is strongly associated with the state. Thus, it is somewhat difficult to comprehend and even to predict its behavior. However, most people have realized that, despite internal struggles and the popular demand for democracy, the military factor cannot be neglected in the recent mechanisms of political configurations.

Since the early 1990s, a number of military presidents, such as Kérékou of Bénin, who was in power on the etiquette of Marxist-Leninism for 18 years before being re-elected in May 1996, Sassou Nguesso in Congo-Brazzaville with his labor union experience in the *Parti du Travail Congolais*, and Kolingba of the Central African Republic (CAR), lost their presidency through elections. This was an important people's statement against the military and for multipartyism. With the re-emergence of multiparty democracy, are we witnessing a real end or an illusionary exit of militarism from the political affairs of governance in African society? Is there a military coup d'état fatigue in Africa? These questions are too broad and have to be qualified. Are soldiers still interested in capturing state power within the existing popular and social movements. Do the conditions that produced military take over in the 1960s, 1970s and 1980s no longer exist?

There are people who tend to support the view that the recent rise of popular and social movements in Africa is likely to weaken the position of military power in the African decision-making process, resource allocation policy, and control of resources, and that these movements may end the intensity of military coup d'états altogether. That is to say that the level of political consciousness is likely to also reach the military class. Others have advanced the view that generals, colonels, and captains in the armies would be unlikely to intervene in politics if the rules of the elected civilians regimes were clearly articulated and respected by the society at large, and if these regimes also had a significant popular base. The view that elected civilian governments tend to create chaos may motivate the military to come back to power. There is also the view that, despite the intensity of the struggle for democracy in the past seven years or so, soldiers as a social class will continue to resist and fight any promising democracy and popular movements in order to protect their own class interests.

Although the adoption of multiparty democracy has been resisted to various degrees and with using different means and strategies by some African states, such as Côte d'Ivoire, Kenya, Malawi, Nigeria, Sierra Leone until the elections of 1996, the Sudan, Togo, Zaïre, and Zimbabwe, in the end, by 1997 some forms of democratic discourses have re-emerged and reached most parts of the continent. Before the current political changes, most African states, both civilian (one-party state) and military regimes, have been functionally militaristic in their legal behaviour and public policy formulation and implementation. That is to say, they have combined the characteristics of authoritarianism and totalitarianism to pursue their policy objectives. The SAPs and the stabilization policies of the International Monetary Fund (IMF) have been adopted in most cases during military regimes. Thus, these international institutions could not, in the past, be disassociated from the militaristic policy of African states. Certain specific conditions and concrete structures, both locally and internationally, have produced such behaviour. African peripheral capitalism became more consolidated during the military regimes than ever before. A certain level of public discourses related to nationalism also occurred during this period in countries such as the CAR, Uganda, Togo, and Zaïre.

With the rise of the struggle for democracy in Africa, can the rigid militarism of 1970s and 1980s re-emerge and function effectively in Africa without re-creating the conditions and struggles that could lead to the total collapse of the state and society such as occurred in Liberia or Somalia? What ought to be the role of militarism in a context in which people have become poorer than ever before in the post-colonial era and thus have passionately associated democracy with development and social progress?

Since the colonial era, Africa, like other developing societies, has produced several generations of people and power systems who have had different perceptions of their systems of governance, culture, and economies. There are people who were born during the colonial era, which can be characterized as a semi or total *état de siège* ("state of siege"), who come to power today. Most of those people saw the militaristic aspects of the colonial political systems in their raw form. In Africa, nationalists and socialists alike believed that the struggle for decolonization was essentially the struggle for political democracy. This struggle has to have both activist and militaristic dimensions. There are others who were born during the time of colonial reforms. In most cases, these are the generations that have fully acquired the legacy of formal education and are now in power although they are still sharing power, with some people from the former generation (the old politicians, known as the *vieux, dikoumanyi, or Mze*). The generation of young Africans in their thirties have known only either the military regimes, one-party states, or various forms of the struggle for democracy. The new generation, with the exception of a few who have been engaged in the struggle for liberation, tend to define democracy *à l'Européenne* as basically the pursuit of individual rights. The majority of the African population, with the exception of people in countries such as Côte d'Ivoire and Senegal, which have been exceptional in that they have not had any military coup d'états take over state power, have always lived under military dictatorship. These regimes have created their own culture and their own social norms.

Since the beginning of the re-emergence of the struggle for democracy in Africa toward the end of the 1980s, and in some cases even earlier, the generally common understanding was that militarism, as a state phenomenon, and democracy as the people's demand and claim, cannot co-exist given the oppressive economic conditions that most of the people found themselves in. Militarism or military regimes have been associated with underdevelopment, corruption, and aberrant nationalism, like in Zaïre under Mobutu or in Uganda under Idi Amin. Thus, this study of militarism has two aspects: a study of the societal struggle for change and a study of the maintenance of the status quo.

In the 1970s and early 1980s in Africa, the perceptions and ideas of modernization theorists about state- and nation-building still prevailed within the framework of a complicated equation of the advocacy of a strong state, as the most important agency of change versus the so-called weak society. In general, African society was wrongly perceived and defined by modernization theorists as socially weak, philosophically irrational or pre-logical, primordially deterministic, socially and historically backward, and politically naive or childish. This definition, which has become irrelevant within the dependency paradigms and globalization arguments, was based on the well-known assumption that the history of social change and people is philosophically linear and universal. The old modernization theorists and their foreign policy implications in the North emphasized the need in developing countries, especially in Africa, for creating strong institutions that could control societal resources and create common values. What states, with their legal and political institutions, were doing to manage resources autocratically was conceived to be legitimate means for building nations. It was believed, following the European model of development, that the *telos* (the ultimate objective with a sense of direction) of a strong state is the creation of a nation. The notion of legitimacy was very much based on the notion that physical force was necessary for making change. In short, as W. F. Gutteridge indicated, "To describe the African armed forces as the channels of technical modernization and innovation in the sense which armies elsewhere have sometimes proved to be is to ignore the facts" (1975, 10).

A BRIEF HISTORY OF MILITARY COUP D'ÉTATS: WHAT DO SOLDIERS WANT?

The military is the state in uniform with guns, physical forces, and laws. Why does it want to recapture the state power in its own name? It is difficult to know exactly what the soldiers who have been involved in military coup d'états want to accomplish in the state because their operations have always been discrete and no consensus has ever been reached between the people and the military officers in terms of the soldiers' motives and agendas. The low visibility army actions and their hierarchical nature, make the discussion on military regimes vague and general.

African political and socio-economic conditions have produced several types of military or semi-military regimes to be classified as follow:

1. Mobutu/Eyadema types, based on an aberrant or faulty nationalism in which power has been highly centralized.
2. Gaddafi types, which have had a popular ideological base and a strong cultural support.
3. Doe types, which have been based on vengeance but without any ideological base.
4. Sankara types, which have been based on a popular revolutionary dogma but without a strong cultural base.
5. Nigerian types, where class, regionalism, and ethnicity play a vital role in the management of power.

Although this classification is not absolute, it can help us locate the dominant ideological and political tendencies that have shaped the reasons why soldiers make coup d'états. These regimes did not come to power in the same way and with the same internal and external support. For example, Babangida of Nigeria, Mobutu of Zaïre, Sankara of Burkina Faso, Mengistu of Ethiopia, and Siad Barre of Somalia did not capture state power with similar missions. Thus, their challenges to democracy should also vary. However, they do have common goals, which include the rapid implementation of change, the destruction of the existing basis for political challenges, the promotion of some elements of nationalism, and the weakening of civil society.

Despite differences in the way colonial powers organized their colonies based on the specific objective conditions of the milieu, there is a consensus that the colonial states were structurally militaristic and philosophically anti-democratic. The dominant mode of governing was militaristic. Coercion was considered a legitimate means of allocating and distributing resources and creating value systems. The institutions of the state were guarded by soldiers (guns and other physical brutalities) and the policy implementation was done by "stick" rather than by "carrot." Although popular movements and colonial reforms had previously led to multipartyism, in most cases, the newly established African political elites inherited strong militaristic states.

Since African countries earned their nominal political independence, there have been more than 40 military *coup d'états* in Africa. This general situation, in most cases, created the conditions that led to political instability, and those conditions have been rapidly deteriorating in many African countries despite the current prospects for democracy. Why have military *coup d'états* succeeded in some places and not in others?

Why and when did the soldiers capture state power? There are many reasons that can explain why these coup d'états have occurred or why the soldiers have occupied presidential palaces. Only the few most important reasons will be discussed here. These factors must be considered analytically as a set of variables and their dynamics, rather than as a single and autonomous factor, or an independent variable.

Among the most important general causes for the rise of the military in state power in Africa are the brutality associated with the end of the colonial powers; class and power struggles between the elites (civilians and military) as reflected in the ethnic violence, for instance, in countries such as Burundi, the Congo, Nigeria, and Rwanda; the lack of integration of the colonial armies into the newly established armies; Cold War politics (the East and West power struggles) and its *cortège* implications in the process of the creation of client states; and the development of the military as a legitimate national profession. The significance of these factors in a specific national milieu cannot be generalized because the development of each of these factors depends on the dynamics of local politics, the new elite's relations with the former colonial powers and with society, and the nature of the forces involved in social and popular movements toward decolonization. In the case of Nigeria, for example, Julius Ihonvbere explained:

Beyond institutional and personal factors, we can identify, at least in the Nigerian case, the weakness and limited legitimacy of the post-colonial state; the factionalisation and fractionalisation of the dominant classes; ethnic, regional and religious pressures and contradictions; mismanagement, violence, thuggery and corruption; the contradictions of underdevelopment and dependence; the marginalization, impoverishment and pauperization of non-bourgeois forces; and vulnerability to external manipulation. Yet, military intervention in Nigerian politics and the suffocation of civil society must be seen as part of the ongoing class struggles in the country and efforts by the bourgeoisie to hold on the state power and build some degree of hegemony.[1]

Samuel Huntington has argued that "the most important causes of military intervention in politics are not military but political and reflect not the social and organizational characteristics of the military establishment but the political and institutional structure of society" (Huntington, 1968, 194). From both the above position and point of view of organizational theory, African military hierarchal structures and professionalism are causes of militarism. Decalo synthesized that "military intervention in the political realm is viewed as a function of chronic systemic disequilibrium and of the alleged professional characteristics of armies, the precise dimensions of which (as well as their specific ingredients and boiling points) may differ from country to country" (Decalo, 1976, 12). Military *coup d'états* do not start in a political vacuum. The international power struggles between the major ideologies and the international division of labor have, in the past, also played a role in the ways local coup d'états either failed or succeeded to seize and hold power.

Between 1952 and 1980, in most cases, the soldiers replaced either semi-parliamentary or fully parliamentary systems. In 1952 in Egypt the first military *coup d'état* led by General Neguib (a member of the free officers' group) with the *complice* ("complicity") of Gamal Abdel Nasser and Anwar Sadat, occurred when King Farouk was forced out of office and assassinated. Since then, Egypt has been ruled by military officers and semi-civilian coalitions. Periodic elections have not led to the establishment of a civilian government. Nasser, Sadat, and Moubarak have all been trained in military academies. The second military coup d'état, which was followed in 1958 in the Sudan was led by General Abbuda. Despite the existence of cultural and ideological elements of pluralism in the Sudan, the military political culture has been strongly rooted on the dominant elite ruling dogmatism. From Gaffar El Nimeiry (1969) to General Omar Hassan El Bashir, who took power in 1989, the soldiers have consolidated their power in a complicated equation of divide and rule. Mobutu of Zaïre and Doe of Liberia, for example, would not have succeeded without the U.S. State Department. Eyadema of Togo would not have stayed in power until today without France.

Between 1960 and 1970, there were 15 military coup d'états in Africa.[2] Between 1970 and 1980, 11 more military coup d'états were added to the list that started with Idi Amin in 1971 in Uganda; and the following decade started with Samuel Kanyon Doe, who took state power by a violent and bloody military coup d'état from the *guru* of the Americo-Liberian empire in April 1980.

In several countries, the period of civilian-elected government since independence has been very short, in most cases fewer than ten years all together. For instance, since 1963 in Bénin, 1963 and 1967 in Togo, 1961 and 1965 in Zaïre, 1966 in Burkina Faso, 1966 in Ghana, 1966 in Nigeria, 1967 in Sierra Leone, 1968 in Libya, and 1969 in Somalia, elected governments have been nominally ephemeral. In other countries, such as Egypt, Togo, Zaïre, Bénin, Burkina Faso and Mauritania until recently, the military or semi-military regimes have based their power on the loyalty to a personality, notably Mubarak, Eyadema, Mobutu, Kérékou, and Ould Taya respectively. Countries such as Algeria, Burkina Faso, Bénin, the CAR, Ghana, Nigeria, Niger, and Sierra Leone have had, before the recent changes, several successive military regimes replacing each other. Their legacy has generally been reflected in the deteriorating socio-economic conditions they have produced. Burkina Faso and Ghana, for example, were once near total collapse under the military succession as soldiers decided to consolidate their powers. *Kalabule* (or what is called *matabishi* in the Congo) was institutionalized in Ghana as a normal market and bureaucratic practice.

Soldiers in power tend to claim that they come to power to restore law and order, maintain the unity of the country, and restore bureaucratic integrity and honesty. The African civilian regimes have been perceived by soldiers as highly corrupt and corruptible. However, the social and economic conditions that military regimes have created in countries such as Nigeria and Zaïre are worse than those created by any elected civilians.

THE MILITARY AND THE DEMOCRATIC EQUATION

The democratic equation as expressed by popular movements implies the promotion of political freedom in all its ramifications, plus economic rights, or economic prosperity, as reflected in basic human rights. Democracy is defined as a process of actualizing freedom and human equality. For the mass of people, this equation is not a just slogan. People believe that democracy will emancipate them and create conditions for their personal growth and development. Do military regimes care much about this equation and multipartyism?

Starting at the end of the 1980s, and within the existing conditions and popular movements, the armies in most parts of Africa started to lose their own established political space and their legitimacy: they were no longer considered the most powerful agents of modernization and stability. In countries such as Bénin, Nigeria, and Zaïre, independent women's organizations, non-governmental organizations (NGOs), ethnic associations, and civil rights organizations have become the new agents of change and the struggle for democracy. The military's displacement is likely to produce several phenomena within the armies:

1. Soldiers are likely to create a new anti-state role for themselves. This role may be based on the utilization of raw force to maintain the status quo.
2. The soldiers may join the mass of people in struggling for political reforms.
3. The soldiers may become the judges of society in terms of making sure that the state of equilibrium is maintained.

However, it should be noted that, generally and pragmatically, soldiers have much to lose if any form of democracy succeeds. This is an important factor to take into consideration as we analyze the reason why they are coming back on the political scene.

In Zaïre, for instance, between 1990 and 1997, soldiers were constantly on streets, not necessarily for military coup d'état against their generals or to take over state power from Mobutu, but to try to improve their salaries and social security in general. There were two serious mutinies that destroyed the country's already badly mismanaged economy. The low-rank military in Zaïre, especially in the large dilapidated cities, formed groups of gangsters, who organized bands with the main objective of stealing and killing to survive. These groups had some connections with higher military officers who supported and equipped them. In a country where the number of generals was very limited compared to Nigeria, and where most potential military officers to be graded to the rank of generals had been either put in jail, forced to retire, or killed, and where the higher officers had relatively low salaries and benefits (about $300 a month as of July 1996 while the low-rank soldier earned less than $20 a month), the chance of having a successful military coup d'état that did not originate from an internal power struggle was extremely low, though not impossible.

The recent military coup d'états in Gambia in July 1994, and Niger in January 1996, and the mutinies in Guinea-Conakry and the CAR after the presidential and general elections, make us re-think the role of soldiers in politics in the post-Cold War period in Africa. Why have the soldiers been agitating to return to the political scene, which is globally in the process of becoming democratic? It may be difficult to know exactly why Ibrahim Maïnassara took power in Niger. However, the political impasse in Niger can probably help explain some important reasons why the military decided to intervene. The president and prime minister fought for several months over the issue of constitutional power, creating political conditions that could have led to the collapse of state. Democracy was perceived from the military point of view as a temporarily dysfunctional system.

In the CAR, as in Zaïre, the soldiers claimed to have not received their monthly salaries and requested new, adequate military equipment in the barracks and training centers.

In several public conferences in 1992 and 1993 at Cornell University and elsewhere, the author has argued that the soldiers are likely to come back quickly in countries where they, constitutionally and politically, did not go far enough or anywhere within the existing structures of power and the social conditions that they created. In most cases, as testified by the level of the African poverty, those conditions cannot be conducive to the ethos or norms of democratic ideals. The lumpen-proletarianization of the army has created lawlessness that is likely to be a serious threat to any process of democratization in Africa. In Zaïre, for instance, since the early 1990s, low-echelon soldiers have had a salary of less than $10 a month. However, their superiors have enjoyed a relatively higher salary of more than $100 a month. Lumpen-proletarianization of the army means, in this case, that soldiers do not have solid sources of revenue and that they have to struggle to survive. Indeed, they have ceased to be qualified as groups of regular workers. Although other workers, including civil servants, have experienced similar or worse conditions, the control of the instruments of brutalization and death give the soldiers a different bargaining power.

Although some president-generals, like Eyadema of Togo, were temporarily out of the political scene (for several months) before re-organizing their parties and building new coalitions, many of them retained military power during the so-called transition period. The internal contradictions and weakness of civil opposition coalitions like those in Zaïre and, to a certain extent, those in Togo, contributed to their coming back to the political scene quickly and easily. In Zaïre, where the transition did not ever start and the democratic process was literally blocked, Mobutu did not go anywhere far from the structure of power during the national conference. He was still in the center of power and succeeded in capturing the national conference and pushing his agenda through. He retained all power, including the "super-constitutional power." Blaise Compaoré of Burkina Faso, Jerry Rawlings of Ghana, Lansana Conté of Guinea-Conakry, and Ould Taya of Mauritania were very much constitutionally and legally present during this period. They did not relinquish their military power and influence during the so-called transition period in their respective countries. Because of internal struggles and weak social and economic conditions, Sassou Nguesso in the Congo was defeated in the 1991 presidential elections, but his opposition to President Pascal Lissouba was very much militaristic and undemocratic. A democratic opposition party within the liberal democracy is expected to use the court and the parliament to challenge the agenda of the ruling party. In the Congo, on most occasions, guns and other violent means were common tools of Nguesso and his party for challenging the government before recapturing the state in October 1997.

The situation in Mali has been relatively different from that in other African states for several reasons:

1. The democracy movement there has had a strong popular characteristic in its composition and social expressions.
2. The military coup d'état of Amadou Toumani Touré can be defined as a popular military coup d'état in which Moussa Traoré, who had been ruling the country since the 1968 coup d'état that toppled Modibo Keita, was arrested in 1991. Like Samuel Kanyon Doe's coup d'état in Liberia in 1980, Touré's takeover was popularly welcome and massively supported.
3. The degree of anger there was much higher than in many countries because Mali is an extremely poor country.
4. Unlike Nigeria, Mali does not have a large and relatively powerful petty bourgeois class that could ally with the state and block the popular struggle, despite the existence of a small, but tightly enriched and corrupt group, including Moussa Traoré. Thus, Amadou Toumani Touré successfully prepared the transition within the framework of strong popular anger.

Nigeria, as discussed in chapter 3, for many years, Ibrahim Babangida and his military junta had been heavily pressured by civil society to return power to civilian rule with a popularly elected president. As indicated below, he did not go far enough and did not have any strong commitment (unlike Bénin where Mathieu Kérékou accepted the dictum of the national conference) and thus was left with very limited power during the transition period. In fact, Babangida created both his model of democracy and the processes of its implementation and imposed the same on Nigerian society. The road to transition has been extremely tough, dangerous, and unpredictable. He invented the tactic that Julius O. Ihonvbere called the "Domesticating Popular Groups and Opposition Elements." As he said:

The purpose of this tactic is basically to control or domesticate opposition forces and keep the transition program in the hands of conservative, pro-IMF and World Bank elements in the country. The military regime has made it very clear that only persons who believe in the IMF/World Bank program and who promise to continue its on-going programs will be allowed to succeed it. This declaration has alienated those who do not share the government's position and has created suspicion that the regime was likely to manipulate the transition program to achieve its narrow objective. Since the transition program does not involve a genuine empowerment of the people and their organizations and does not involve the structural transformation of society, it has become inevitable that popular forces, trade unionists, students, civil liberty organizations, social critics, and those Babangida calls "extremists" are kept under control.[3]

Compared to other countries where the institutions to support the transition have been lacking, the Nigerian government produced a good number of such institutions, such as the National Electoral Commission, the Constitution Drafting Committee, the Directorate of Mass Mobilization for Social Justice and Economic Recovery, and the Transition to Civil Rule Tribunal, to support the transition.[4] However, Babangida's military regime did not allow the democratic transition to have its own autonomy and grow. After nullifying the result of the presidential elections and creating political confusion in the country, the November 1993 military coup d'état of Abacha and his brutalities eloquently show how far the military regime can go in Nigeria. Although General Abacha, the number-two man after Babangida, has set up some transition programs to organize the elections, the increase in political assassinations, hidden under the guise of armed robbery, has become a direct means for the military regime to continuously destroy the basis for democracy.

The Nigerian military as a social class has consolidated its power and has also continuously polarized civil society, which is itself weak because most of its leaders cannot survive independently from the state's resource base and affiliations. Nigeria, as is the case in most African countries, has not yet produced a national bourgeoisie that is productively autonomous from the state in terms of both its economic capabilities and political base. Nigeria is perhaps the only country in Africa where a considerable number of generals and other high ranking officials within the armed forces are forced or decide to retire while they are still young and, in some cases, very young. These generals enter the business sphere with the support of the military apparatus and the political culture. In most cases, they use military channels to facilitate their national and international transactions. This behavior is not unique to Nigeria. However, Nigeria has a larger and stronger class of military petty bourgeoisie than other countries in Africa. Unlike Ethiopia and Zaïre, which have also had an important number of military officers in the 1970s and 1980s, the military petty bourgeois class in Nigeria is deeply involved in local and national politics. This, for example, has not been the case in Bénin, Ghana, and Togo.

The military regimes in Africa have a history of human rights abuses. With a few exceptions, such as Sankara of Burkina Faso, the military regimes in Africa do not question the foundation of the African state, its laws, and its relationship with the society. They do not see themselves as being part of society. This attitude is partially due to the tendency of soldiers to define the state as the supra-society entity. Soldiers do not define themselves as being part of the citizenry. Bokassa, Eyadema, Doe, and Mobutu have often behaved as though they were identical to, or more powerful than, the state and society. From this perspective, the foundation of the democratic equation based on the rights of citizens to enjoy liberties and economic rights, has been constantly violated. This violation was also due to the militarization of African society, which has created a culture that almost legitimizes the use of force or corruption to obtain services and influence opinions. In the 1970s Mobutu of Zaïre preached with pride his dogma of stealing with prudence. The pillage that took place in Zaïre was directly related to this freedom of corruption scheme that Mobutu produced. For instance, despite the Nigerians' hatred for military regimes (which exists for similar reasons in Togo and Zaïre), the militaristic behavior of Nigerians within the bureaucracy and in the market place is a testimony of how militaristic culture has been embodied in the national culture.

NOTES

1. Julius O. Ihonvbere, "Military and Political Engineering under Structural Adjustment: The Nigerian Experience Since 1985," *Journal of Political and Military Sociology* 20 (Summer 1991): 107.

2. For further information on the subject, see the article of Badara Diouf on "Coup d'Etat: Panorama d'un phénomene inquiétant," *Le Soleil* (newspaper), Vendredi, 14 juin 1996 (Dakar, Senegal): 9.

3. Ihonvbere, "Military and Political Engineering," 118.

4. Ibid, p. 110.

7

Structural Adjustment Programs and Their Implications in the Struggle for Democracy

INTRODUCTION

Recently a great deal has been written about the impact of the Structural Adjustment Programs (SAPs), especially their microeconomics. Because the new World Bank president, James Wolfensohn, seems to have a special interest in Africa, studies on the SAPs are likely to increase. In 1997, he declared that "Africa is World Bank's top priority."[1] This priority commitment has been repeated in 1998. Most earlier studies on the SAPs were conducted and published in the North. With few exceptions, these studies have been neo-classical, ahistorical, and they have focused on the monetaristic and technical dimensions of the Bank's role. Moreover, they relegated the dynamics of local realities to a low analytical level. The intent in this chapter is to raise certain philosophical issues about the SAPs and their impact on the current multiparty democracy in an African context.[2]

Between the 1970s and the early 1990s, three phenomena—the adoption of the SAPs of the World Bank and the stabilization programs of the International Monetary Fund (IMF), the rise of the struggle for multiparty democracy, and a movement towards "de-statization" (meaning de-construction of the state) and marginalization of Africa—have characterized the dynamics of African society. In a fragile and unpredictable transition, relationships between these phenomena are complex because each of them represents a different perspective on how Africa should be defined and how it should function. Furthermore, each has its own ethos, worldview, and constituency. Thus, this transition is itself epistemologically a problematical because it offers neither a viable developmental alternative nor the needed philosophical foundation for policy formulation and implementation. During the Cold War, conventional paradigms about development and democracy were mainly framed within the ideologies of liberalism, scientific socialism, and third worldism. As stated previously, Third worldism was dominated by dependency theory, which is associated with either Gunder Frank, or Cardoso, or Samir Amin and their followers. However, most of these paradigms did not go far enough in explaining African conditions and politics because they tended to put more emphasis on the international determinism of the metropolitan political actors and their institutions.

This chapter discusses the impact of the SAPs on both state efforts (or lack of efforts) for planning and on the objectives of the struggle for multiparty democracy. The dynamics of the SAPs and the movements for multiparty democracy in Africa must be studied structurally and historically to understand the nature of their implications in a comprehensive manner. The first part of this chapter presents the issues to be covered; the second part briefly examines African conditions and the SAPs' objectives; the third part deals with the dynamics of state's dynamics and the SAPs' political philosophy of planning; the fourth part deals with the assumptions behind the struggle for multiparty democracy and the assumptions of the SAPs; and the fifth part presents a short conclusion. Issues are identified and questions raised about the SAPs and about democratic ideals and movements. Many parts in this section have been discussed before, but they are used in this context as references for a critical assessment purpose.

In Africa, the role of the SAPs and their privatization has been more publicized than similar innovations of other international programs. This is no accident. Within the world system, since World War II, the SAPs have had more visibility and real political leverage in influencing politics and policies in Africa than any other program. There are four reasons why these programs are vital to world politics:

1. They are designed in the metropolitan center (the center of world power).
2. Their supportive institutions and states preceive them to be ideologically and politically neutral.
3. They are perceived as the universal and benevolent savior of the African state.
4. They are authoritative and have technical abilities to deliver services faster than other programs. Thus, SAPs are perceived to be the most reliable external intervening factor in Africa.

Despite real and potential contradictions, the role of the IMF and the World Bank is likely to increase in 21st-century Africa because the industrial nations, the providers of financial capital and technologies, have decided to empower those institutions as the major decision makers in the financial sectors and in the development agenda. In 1995, the World Bank directly or indirectly stands on "the critical path" of nearly 75 percent of the capital flow and debt relief to Africa (Lione, 1995, 8). This responsibility, and the conditions surrounding its actualization, can positively or negatively change the role of the World Bank and the IMF. If democratic pluralism, or multipartyism, become legitimized through popular political and social participation, the World Bank and the IMF, despite their power, can be forced to adopt reforms framed with democratic ideals. If they don't, these organizations may become partially dysfunctional. However, if challenges to the SAPs from the bottom are fully consolidated, institutions of power in the North, in collaboration with states both in the North and the South, may intervene to crush the movements of the struggle for democracy. One of the common characteristics of the democratic struggle, one which may threaten the SAPs, is the citizens' quest for full participation in the affairs of state and society. "Autonomization" of regions or provinces, as pursued by the democratic struggle in some countries, can also challenge the SAPs' policies. Citizens' political rights to elect their representatives, to influence policy input, and to make policy choices individually or collectively cannot be disassociated from state planning for the future.

Since their inception and adoption in the early 1980s in Africa, SAPs and the stabilization programs have been controversial in terms of their design, their implementation approach, their social and political implications, and their underlying philosophical and teleological assumptions. To some they brought a high level of optimism at a time of generalized economic crisis. To others, they brought a high level of skepticism concerning the development strategy that Africans should follow. Even the World Bank itself has no clear intellectual or philosophical consensus about evaluating the long-term impact of its African programs. However, despite controversies and much resistance to their agenda, as of 1997, more than 40 African states have partially or fully adopted the SAPs and IMF stabilization programs. Many still need access to the resources of the bank and their affiliated institutions. Thus, it is clear that the World Bank and the IMF are perceived by many African states as be necessary evils.

World Bank advocates argue that if the SAPs have succeeded in improving living standards in some countries in South America and Asia (before the recent financial crisis), there are no apparent logical or historical reasons why they should not succeed in Africa. From this point of view, and without asking what the criteria of success are, the initial African conditions before the adoption of the SAPs have been evaluated mainly on the basis of the African state's abilities or inabilities to adopt the "universal" characteristics of the world economy. Those advocates also believe in the Keynesian assumption that a country that spends and borrows enough can eliminate poverty. Thus, it must be asked: Are the reforms pursued by the bank, under pressure from many international and national organizations since the 1980s, permanent?

MAJOR CLAIMS AND OBJECTIVES OF THE STRUCTURAL ADJUSTMENT PROGRAMS

In the past 16 years or so, the SAPs have had different names or labels and different interpretations, all of which makes understanding them more difficult in terms of specifying the nature of their impact. As stated in a report of the Committee on Foreign Affairs of the United States House of Representatives: "In response to the African economic crisis of the 1980s, international donors have been reforming their assistance programs, spawning a rapid and confusing succession of labels: 'stabilization,' 'adjustment,' 'economic policy reforms,' 'structural adjustment,' 'sector adjustment with a human face, etc."[3]

This name changing is not random: it has strategic and functional meanings. Since the 1980s, when the SAPs and the stabilization policies of the IMF were adopted by the African states, these programs and their derivative policies have not been fully accepted even by their own national supporters in Africa. Through these programs and policies, there has been a systematic effort to re-integrate Africa into the world economy through the market. However, the translation of the claimed successes of the SAPs into adequate living standards for the majority of the people and real benefits for the society at large have been much debated. This is so because, since the 1980s, after the adoption of the SAPs, the social conditions of most people have not qualitatively improved. As Nancy E. Wright describes the situation:

The 1980s were disastrous for sub-Saharan Africa. Per capita income was lower at the end of the decade than at the beginning, and a host of other social indicators—infant mortality rates, per capita calorie intake, number of students enrolled in primary and secondary schools—all suggest that the continent made no progress or slipped in the effort to alleviate social ills. (1990, 21)

Yet Edward Jaycox, then World Bank vice president for Africa, concluded in his 1994 report that about 15 African countries have improved their policies and reaped gains in higher rates of growth; moreover, between 1987 and 1991, there was a median improvement of 1.8 percent points in the growth rate of the per capita gross domestic product (GDP) and an improvement in GDP per capita of 1.1 percent.[4] As noted by Mengisteab and Logan:

The IMF and the World Bank, the principal sponsors and implementers of the economic adjustment in Africa, argue that the strategies have already produced considerable positive results. The Bank claimed, for example, that the economies of adjusting sub-Saharan countries grew at the rate of 4 percent during the period of 1988–90, compared to 2.2 per cent for non-adjusting countries. (1995, 1)

This view was echoed by Pierre Landell-Mills, a World Bank official, who claims that structural adjustment has worked where it has been undertaken on a sustained basis. He cited, for instance, Guinea-Conakry and Ghana, which have grown at a rate of 5 to 6 percent per year, and Madagascar, which has grown from -2 to 2 percent a year. He also notes how two economic recovery programs, from 1984 to 1986 and from 1987 and 1989, reduced inflation in Ghana.[5]

Reasons why the African state adopted them and they continue to perceive them as necessary programs for their functioning are both general and specific. Pressures from international financial institutions to create rigid common guidelines for loans, resettle financial disputes, and re-organize aid policies; the disabilities of the national economies in their performance; their strategies of accumulation of surpluses and their policies of attracting foreign capital; and the change in the structures of the world economy are all factors that have forced Africa to adopt these programs, which are perceived by some as Africa's "savior."

The mission of the World Bank and the IMF has already been well-defined, discussed, publicized, and established. They are diversified organizations, and their programs have not been similarly adopted at once in all countries. In all cases, their implementation has been gradual. For the purpose of this study, they need only be summarized by the following goals: to implement measures to stop economic decline and improve the general performance of a country's economy, and to assist in assessing budget deficits and imbalances in trade through packages of corrective measures. Most of the adjustment programs in Africa contain varying degrees of corrective policies focusing on currency devaluation of the currency, stabilization of interest rates, reduction of government expenditures to make them into line with real resources, privatization, liberalization, and institutional reform.[6] Exchange rate policy is supposed to act to devalue currency so that export commodities can become cheaper and more attractive to foreign buyers. Terms of trade are expected to be fully liberalized to improve the movement of goods, and fiscal policies are supposed to remove tax and tariff barriers. Interest rate policies are undertaken to encourage the population to save money and to tighten credit so that people borrow less. The government is encouraged to cut spending on subsidies and other services.

In short, generally, adjustment programs include reforms to

* establish a market-determined exchange rate
* bring fiscal deficits under control
* liberalize trades
* improve the financial sector, the efficiency of public enterprises, and the coverage and quality of social services

World Bank officials continue to argue that the main factors behind Africa's stagnation and decline have been poor macroeconomic and sectoral policies, emanating from a development paradigm that gave the state a prominent role in regulating economic activity.[7] In a recent policy report, the World Bank stated: "Overvalued exchange rates and large and prolonged budget deficits undermined the macroeconomic stability needed for long-term growth. Protectionist trade policies and government monopolies reduced the competition so vital for increasing productivity" (1990, 20).

Liberalization of the market, efficient management of state resources, and further integration of the African economies into the global economy are the most important dogmatic elements of the systematic theology of the World Bank.

Most of the World Bank's studies have been dominated by functionalist scholars, who focus mainly on the monetaristic, institutional, and technical dimensions of the role of the World Bank, relegating the role and forces of the local situation to a secondary analytical level. Within this framework, initial and objective African conditions have not been taken seriously. World Bank's studies still use ahistorical Rostowian logic and stages of development that have been perceived as universal or Western-dominated paradigms.[8]

The impact and implications of the SAPs should be located within the perspective of the dynamic of global capitalism and its paradigmatic and policy assumptions and contradictions, and the forces of the local realities must be taken into account. The popular tendencies of proclaiming the World Bank and the IMF to be the only sources of African economic and social maladies are not intellectually and politically accurate because they are not supported by the before-adjustment policy data and political histories. In short, despite some shifts in World Bank thinking in recent years—for instance, the emphasis on rural poverty "alleviation," capacity building, education, and women's issues—reliance on market forces remains the key element of the World Bank's policy prescription.

THE AFRICAN CONDITIONS

Current African socio-economic, cultural, and political conditions cannot be defined in monolithic and ahistorical terms, for they have been produced by the interplay of local and international configurations of power, class struggles, and diverse internal dynamics. Moreover, they are dependent on the evolution of world capitalism, the impact of the end of the Cold War, the behavior of the state, ruling elite, and the nature of the specific African society. However, the characteristics of the classical role of Africa as a market, within the global political economy, can be generalized. Within the current productive conditions of synthetic materials and high competitive technologies in the global system, the role of Africa as a consumer has been considerably reduced. Thus, although African conditions are heavily influenced by local and regional realities, their characteristics have a similar ideological and functional significance across political regimes in the international economy.

While the percentage of GDP devoted to consumption has risen, the low absolute levels of per capita GDP do not translate these increases into an expanding market. In comparison, 1993 per capita GDP was $18,060 for the United Kingdom and $24,700 for the United States. Moreover, most African nations experienced declining percentages of GDP devoted to investment and savings, and rising external debt. The average per capita GDP was less than $400.00. This makes one wonder about the sustainability of current consumption patterns.

The causes of the African crisis must be understood as cumulative and multidimensional, and they can be localized or centralized within the world economy. The oil shocks of 1973 and 1974 and 1978 and 1979 can be considered, among other factors, as one of the leading causes of the crisis. Moreover, the collapse in the world prices of primary commodities, including coffee, cotton, copper, cocoa, tea, sisal, and oil, is one of the most important causes of the African crisis.

These commodities account for more than 80 percent of Africa's exports. Ecological disasters caused by bad weather and droughts have seriously impacted more than 20 countries. In addition, the effects of the politics of nationalization or Africanization on the national economies in the 1970s in countries such as Tanzania, Zambia, Congo-Zaïre, the Sudan, and Uganda were economically devastating because of mismanagement and lack of planning. Nevertheless, this was politically important for the consolidation of power by the ruling class.

By the 1980s, African conditions have become worse than they were in the 1960s. Per capita agricultural output has stagnated or declined; industrial output has fallen; deforestation and desertification have reduced the availability of productive land; food imports have risen in almost all of Africa; and declining terms of trade predominates. Indeed, between 1977 and 1985, the GDP per capita fell by 15 percent, and Africa's share of poverty was projected to double between 1985 and 2000, and African women living in poverty reached nearly 50 percent in 1980.

Moreover, the African economy is highly fragmented for several reasons: the small size of its domestic economy, the low volume of trade among African countries, and its unidimensional relations with industrial countries. About 85 percent of the continent's total exports are marketed with industrialized countries of the North (compared to 75 percent for South America and 68 percent for South and East Asia). Only a very small fraction of African exports (3 to 6 percent), goes to other African countries. About 30 African countries are landlocked; most of these are situated more than 1,000 kilometers from any seaport. In general, African economic performance has lagged in comparison to other developing countries with relatively similar conditions. For instance, from 1982 to 1992, the average annual GDP growth for Africa was only 2 percent; for South Asia, the most comparable region, it was a little over 5 percent, while for Southeast Asia, it was 8 percent (Callaghy, 1994, 31).

In the late 1980s, many African countries were faced with a negative growth syndrome, and their national economies were near partial or total collapse. Economic growth has been minimal in many of these countries in the early 1990s: generally, it has been between 1.0 and 3 percent, while the population growth has averaged between 3.0 to 3.5 percent.

African conditions can also be defined in terms of strong state interventionism. Since liberal democracy was introduced in the early 1960s without creating its supportive institutions and culture, only a few African states actually implemented it. In most cases, a liberal economy was maintained without liberal politics, and state interventionism was a common political strategy to deal with the inherited problems of post-colonial society. During this period, nationalism and socialism had strange marriages in terms of policy choices and political organizations.Kwame Nkrumah of Ghana and Julius Nyerere of Tanzania were among those leaders who were trying to promote both nationalism and socialism in their public discourses, although their policy base did not reflect strong nationalistic and socialistic foundations. They attempted to adopt some elements of the planned economy. First of all, in the conventional literature, planning is about problem solving (Dyckman, 1975). Within current African conditions, planning essentially means imagining or searching for mechanisms to alleviate or eliminate poverty.

The first step in this direction is to understand poverty and its causes. In general terms, a planned economy within African Marxist regimes, a liberal market within military regimes, and one-party states were the dominant models between 1960 and 1980. However, the choice of a given political leader adopting a given policy based on a selected ideology did not matter much for the people. For them, whatever system seemed to work was more important than its ideological connotations. By the end of the 1970s, African conditions showed signals of a generalized malaise because many domestic policies had not qualitatively changed since the states gained their independence. Restructuring their economies was an urgent developmental need. Given these conditions, what kind of restructuring is needed in most cases?

Concern is to identify the philosophical assumptions behind World Bank and IMF power relations, the objectives of which have been defined and discussed in many studies. The book only intends to shed light on a few of their main features. Elliot Berg has broadly defined the SAPs as the adoption of measures that would make an economy more productive, flexible, and dynamic, by more efficient use of available resources, and by the generation of new resources. The World Bank implemented measures to reverse economic decline and stimulate growth. The IMF stabilization programs were intended to control budget deficits and trade imbalances through packages of currency devaluation, interest rate adjustments, reduction of government expenditures, trade liberalization, and institutional reforms (World Bank, 1990, 1). These programs and policies were recommended to the state and its agencies to achieve fiscal equilibrium, sustainable current account deficits, and a reduction in the rate of inflation. Of course, the government is encouraged to cut spending on subsidies and on other services, especially those that support the poor.

In 1994, the World Bank continued to argue that the main factors for Africa's stagnation and decline have been poor macro-economic and sectoral policies, emanating from a development paradigm that gave a prominent role to regulating economic activity (World Bank, 1994, 3). It also reported that "overvalued exchange rates and large and prolonged budget deficits undermined the macro-economic stability needed for long-term growth. Protectionist trade policies and government monopolies reduce the competition so vital for increasing productivity" (World Bank, 1994, 20).

In short, liberalization of the market, efficient management of state resources, and further integration of the African economies into the global economy have become the most important elements of the Bank's dogmatism. The market and its forces remain the key elements in the bank's restructuring and in its policy prescriptions.

It should be mentioned that the adoption and implementation of the SAPs in Africa in have so far generally produced mixed results and consequences in different sectors of the economies and societies, and in different political periods, among various social classes, countries, and states. Any efforts at generalization and homogenization can be misleading. Given the nature of the African state, how does it work with the invisible hand of Adam Smith?

However, by any standard, including that of the World Bank itself, general African conditions have considerably degraded: in many sectors, in many countries, and among many social groups, they have become worse between the 1980s and the early 1990s than they were in the 1960s. Indeed, the level of poverty is sharply increasing. As stated earlier, as of 1996, there were an estimated 300 million poor African people out of, a total population of, about 625 million. Among these 300 million as of 1997 about 210 million are estimated to be extremely poor, most of whom are women. This estimation uses many combined criteria such as savings, malnutrition, lack of access to land (and productive conditions) and to basic necessities, low daily intake of calories, and low literacy rate.

Given these conditions of poverty, identifying and understanding the causes of the African maladies, and discovering these maladies' cures, have continued to preoccupy scholars and policy makers.

THE AFRICAN STATE AND THE SAPs

African states' demand for, and response to, the SAPs should be examined within the logic of the international political economy and national dynamics. Both external and internal factors have played a role in the way SAPs have been adopted. Colonial and post-colonial states in Africa have common characteristics: both are products of international power struggles and are, therefore, international institutions *par excellence*. They were organized to be powerful institutions, and their mission was to create nations. To advance this objective, the post-colonial state, with the support of multinationals and powerful states in the North, in internal power consolidation. The consequent militarization must be analyzed within the framework of Cold War ideologies. These states had an obligation first to satisfy the requirements of the equilibrium of the international economy for its own survival. This by itself is a strong reason why the adoption of the SAPs can be considered essential for maintenance of the status quo. Yet satisfaction of the SAP criteria drained wealth from the nation that was needed to fuel internal development. Two periods can be distinguished in the development of the African states and their economies, whose differences are more functional than structural and philosophical.

The first is the period of the euphoria of nationalism and the second is the militarization of the African state and politics. Instead of creating new mechanisms for national planning within the state apparatus, many nationalist leaders decided to separate the political struggle from the economic struggle. For instance, the political elite in the former French colonies decided to remain under the protection and shadow of the French economy. Strong ties in the form of economic, military, political, and cultural cooperation were conceived as ways to push national planning toward some indeterminate future. With various strategies, similar arrangements were made by African states within the Commonwealth. Furthermore, some African countries were born without any central banks or ministries of planning to regulate the movements of trade and currency. In these cases, metropolitan banks both in the colonies and Europe, which mostly work for their own interests, were used for that purpose. For instance, *Crédit Lyonnais* in France, *Banque Lambert* in Belgium, and Barclay Bank in England played vital roles in the process of the state amorphous planning in many parts of Africa.

The struggle for forms of political independence that do not link international economics with the social demands of national politics is one of the common discourses of the post-colonial state. Some states, such as Algeria, Tanzania, and Guinea-Bissau, decided, based on their own struggles, to adopt the principles of a planned economy. However, even here the elite were capable of hijacking the planning process.

In general, the nationalists in power pursued what can be characterized as the Africanization of capitalism and socialism. They attempted to make these two ideologies more relevant within African conditions but without necessarily adopting their institutional framework or decision-making philosophies. In the case of both capitalism and socialism, the state did not adequately develop internal planning mechanisms. The systematic refusal of the African state to behave as socialist or capitalist in terms of planning and public management is an indication of its eclectic nature. Thus, the African states became peripheral to both capitalist and socialist management systems, and national planning efforts were relegated to the secondary bureaucratic echelon. Within a highly dependent economy, constrained by the world capitalist system in general, and the SAPs in particular, the national planning units became dysfunctional. The African state did not control the elements needed for appropriate planning, and lacked a strong political will to create its own planning philosophy.

The second period is characterized by the rise of militarization, when new actors joined the African petty bourgeoisie. As discussed in chapter 6, in contrast to the civilian elements of this petty bourgeoisie, who had some national agenda, the soldiers had little, if any, national vision (with a few exceptions, such as Sankara of Burkina Faso and Murtala Muhammad of Nigeria). Indeed, the military's claim generally has been that they must re-establish discipline, law and order. The domain of state planning and resource management became problematic. Without such mechanisms, it is easy to deplete national resources and remain in power with guns. The example of Kaduna Mafia in Nigeria and Mobutuism in Zaïre are telling. Toward the end of the 1970s, most African people had lost the hope that had been articulated in the discourses of independence, and the crisis of the state's legitimacy was manifest in its unreliability. The symptoms of this crisis included the state's incapacity to deliver services, its institutional weaknesses, a lack of political philosophy and confidence to guide its policies, and a high level of dependency on the former colonial powers.

For the World Bank, the disarticulation of the African economies can be defined in terms of a fiscal crisis, declining terms of trade, and mismanagement. When the SAPs were introduced, international institutions and states in the North believed that efficient management of fiscal policies would create conditions for national planning and economic growth. Frankly, the SAPs were first introduced to manage the crisis, not to fuel development. The politics of planning that emerged from interactions between the SAPs and the African states must be addressed.

The SAPs were introduced in four major stages between 1981 and 1995. The first was from 1981 and 1984, and its main target was to attain macro-economic balance by bringing national expenditures into line with national revenues. The second stage, from 1984 and 1986, emphasized the more efficient allocation of resources by switching resources across economic sectors. The third phase, from 1987–1992, underlined the process of mobilizing more resources, as opposed to raising rates of economic growth and living standards for the poor. In the fourth period, from 1992 and 1994, the focus was on poverty alleviation and capacity building. As of 1995, poverty alleviation, capacity-building, rural development, and women issues had become very much a part of the new World Bank's global project for Africa. Although the above classification is certainly simplified, it illustrates the changes in priorities and global objectives of the bank. Within these priorities and objectives, what is the place of national planning?

While the bank has its own planning scheme and development project for Africa, it has been working with the African states, many of which have not consistently developed clear national planning. Hypothetically, states that have a relatively stronger national planning base, and had consistent policies prior to the SAPs, would be likely to do better than those that simultaneously use the SAPs as planning and development devices. For instance, Ghana, Mauritius, Zimbabwe, had some institutional planning before the adoption of the SAPs. Thus, the outcome of the SAPs in those countries are likely to be different from that in the countries that were politically and ideologically bankrupt and administratively dysfunctional before the adoption of SAPs, such as Liberia, the Sudan, and Congo-Zaïre. That is, a country's initial political and economic conditions make its adoption of SAPs vary from other countries.

What is the status of the SAPs in 1998? Many reforms have been announced by the bank to rethink about its new relationship with the states and the NGOs in Africa. The bank has undertaken a major study of poverty in many African countries. Some of its policies are likely to change with the new findings. Most African states have been pursuing their SAPs with agony and cynicism. In 1995, the bank celebrated 40 years of existence with optimism and pride. In the bank's 1994 report, 6 of 26 African countries (Ghana, Tanzania, the Gambia, Burkina-Faso, Nigeria, and Zimbabwe), which have consistently and comprehensively implemented the SAPs since 1981, were claimed to have improved their macro-economic policies. Nine other countries (Madagascar, Malawi, Burundi, Kenya, Mali, Mauritania, Senegal, Niger, and Uganda) were characterized as having experienced modest improvement. The last 11 countries (Bénin, the Central African Republic, Rwanda, Sierra Leone, Togo, Zambia, Mozambique, the Congo, Côte d'Ivoire, Cameroon, and Gabon), experienced an overall deterioration in their macro-economic policies. Some of the countries in this final category have been praised for their particular efforts to implement SAPs in some areas, such as tax collection.

Using the three criteria of fiscal policy, monetary policy, and exchange rate, Edward Jaycox, the then World Bank's vice president for Africa, concluded that the SAPs have worked well because (1) about 15 African countries have improved their policies and reaped gains in higher rates of growth; and (2) between 1987 and 1991, there was a median improvement of 1.8 percent in the growth rate of the per capita gross domestic product (GDP) and an improvement in an average GDP per capita of 1.1 percent. In the same report, Jaycox emphasized that the SAPs should not be a substitute for strong investment programs, capacity-building, and better public policy management—the essential elements of any national planning. Thus, it must be asked whether a state can pursue its policy and adopt the SAPs within the context of the rise of democratic nationalism.

POPULAR AND MULTIPARTY DEMOCRATIC MOVEMENTS AND THE SAPs' ASSUMPTIONS

Some scholars pose serious questions concerning the linear relationship between development and democracy. Despite a lack of consistent empirical data to support such assumptions in specific cases in Africa, most students of development agree that there cannot be any broad development until people fully participate in the process of its construction or re-construction. As the late Claude Ake told the author in a conversation:

Democracy requires even development, otherwise it cannot give equal opportunities to all; it cannot incorporate all to articulate their interests to negotiate them. It cannot produce a political community in which all are able to enjoy rights, nor avoid compromising justice. This is why development in this broad sense is an integral part of the process of democratization.

Popular movements and multiparty politics, which demand openness, power sharing, and fair distribution of resources, are seriously challenging the power, policies, and legitimacy of African states. Although this challenge may not be ideological, it is forcing the state to make some concessions. This leads to further questions. Can multipartyism, as currently defined and practiced in Africa, produce both genuine democracy and social progress? Moreover, what is the difference between multiparty politics in former one-party states such as Bénin, Burkina Faso, Cameroon, the Congo, Kenya, Malawi, Nigeria, and Togo?

The majority of Africans, especially the poor, have been alienated from the state. In countries like the Sudan, Sierra Leone , and Congo-Zaïre, most people are in a "state of nature" or have become resigned to being poor. Resources are becoming less available, and the state has become more selective in managing its citizens' business, even within the framework of existing democratic movements. Furthermore, political instability has not allowed development of individual initiative. Animosity toward the state is a function of the relationship between people's expectations of what the state ought to do and the actual performance of the state. The excessive use of power by a small elite to articulate their own interests, coupled with an increase in poverty, created uncommunicated and uneasy relations among the state, the peripheral capitalist political economy, and the people. The process of internationalization of labor, the accumulation of surpluses, the control of resources by multinationals, the power struggle between the North and South, and the crisis of peripheral capitalism (as reflected by its failures to deliver) must also be taken into account as factors that led to the rise of popular movements.

Popular movements, defined as coalitions of various movements and organizations, articulate social and political issues, generally in non-ideological terms. They have the potential to advance history, although not necessarily toward a concrete national or social revolutionary objective. In some countries popular uprisings have led to the collapse of regimes (for example, Ghana, Mali, and the Sudan). The Moi government in Kenya was likewise challenged by political opposition and popular movements in the early 1990s.

These movements often act spontaneously without having a strong ideological basis. Nevertheless, they are capable of creating momentum toward a long-term struggle for change. In Africa, they are often led and organized by strong, charismatic leaders who tend to become idolized. Their effectiveness does not depend on the strength of their institutions and organizations; rather, it relies on the leader's personality to mobilize people. They contribute to the current processes of political change by creating space in which the state and society can enter into a dialogue. Although these movements in most cases have not brought down the current regimes, they have contributed to demystifying and weakening their power bases and public images. This has been accomplished through their demands for equal distribution of national resources, more participation in the affairs of the society, protection of basic human and social rights, and ecological reforms, distribution of land, power sharing, and job development. The objectives of these movements are philosophically in conflicts with the SAPs' general purposes. The SAPs' functioning assumptions are essentially based on an economistic logic. From the point of view of popular movements in Africa, democracy is defined first of all, as a people's social phenomenon (Mahmood Mamdani and Wamba-dia-Wamba, 1995). Until recently, the perception of development within the SAPs has been very much economistic, technical, and not social. The World Bank and the IMF have become the champions of multipartyism as a means to promote the SAPs. What is the real function and significance of multipartyism?

As defined earlier, multipartyism is an expression of political pluralism within a liberal democracy. Moreover, it is a political situation embedded in a given constitutional arrangement, in which a political elite is forced to allow several functioning political parties to compete for legislative and presidential offices. In this context, civil society becomes a potential instrument of policy formation and, consequently, of social progress. In theory, multipartyism offers several options as to for how to govern and how to be governed.

The key issues in African political pluralism should be the distribution of power and resource management, and their policy implications. Poverty is the foremost African problem, and the issue of equity is an important ethical assumption within the analysis of multipartyism and democracy. The majority of Africans tend to perceive democracy in ethical and developmental terms. Multipartyism is not a strong instrument for structural changes if a democracy does not include accountability, respect for the right to life, social equality, and collective responsibility. Conceptually, democracy may be more valuable for the people than multipartyism. Thus, as previously discussed, political pluralism should not simply be defined as a descriptive, technical expression of Dahl's pluralistic elite theory. Rather, it is a mixture of both a normative and prescriptive phenomenon.

The vital remaining issue is whether or not the structures and political economy of the neo-colonial African state can create conditions conducive to genuine social democracy and institutional planning. What is the significance of freedom and human rights without economic self-sufficiency? What do popular elections of leaders mean to such poor people?

Historically and philosophically, no country, people, or nation has succeeded in acquiring democracy in meaningful social and economic ways without first becoming politically independent. This independence cannot be earned without cultural, political, and economic struggle. Recently, the struggle against the SAPs policies has been organized by rural women, students, formal political and social organizations, and working classes. The permanent lumpen-proletarians, the unpaid workers, and women and men from the informal sector, have also taken to the streets to protest state policies. The spontaneous coalitions that have arisen among these different social classes, though fragile, have produced popular movements.

The struggle for democracy in Africa cannot be reduced only to the struggle for state power or control of the state's resources as generally perceived by some students of politics. Rather, it is the right to live well in one's social milieu and the right to determine what is good or bad within one's social environment. The search for a value system is a struggle for democracy, representing the people's effort to disengage from outmoded neo-colonial state programs and the SAPs' agendas. Thus, democracy should be defined as a human rights issue.

The implementation of the SAPs has not promoted the practices of democracy as a human rights issue. This is due partially to the fact that the SAPs' objectives and those of the states and the people have been antagonistically defined and pursued to for different ends, which are also not necessarily complementary. Although the austerity programs have stabilized some aspects of the state's fiscal activities (such as tax collection) and stimulated growth in some export sectors in some countries such as the Côte d'Ivoire and Ghana, they also have seriously destabilized household financial and economic foundations and the base for individual planning. Cuts in agricultural subsidies, decreases in salaries, currency devaluation, and growth of the lumpen-proletarian class in the urban areas, have sharpened social class tensions and frustrations. Thus, in Bénin, Côte d'Ivoire, Ghana, Algeria, Cameroon, Congo, RDC, Mali, Zambia, and recently in Zimbabwe, workers and academics have been constantly in the streets to force governments to change some of policies that negatively affect purchasing power. As previously indicated, this confrontational approach has challenged the ethos and practices of multipartyism. Indeed, in most cases, this situation is likely to lead to further political instability and social violence.

In short, a real democratic right is essentially a development right. In this context, development is not narrowly defined as an increase in per capita income. A broader concept of development, that incorporates basic civil and political freedoms, implies a democracy which insures these freedoms. In this broad sense, democracy is more conducive to authentic development than is a non-democratic regime.

During the Cold War era, the instruments of development and the policies articulated by the African states were heavily influenced by the international power struggle between the United States and the former Soviet Union. However, popular movements and struggles for democracy should not neglect the international context in which they are operating. If left alone, could Africa take care of its malaise via its own means? Can democracy be taken seriously at the local and national level without having economic correspondence at the international level?

Current democratic discourses are mainly concerned with power, the mechanisms of its production and reproduction, the processes of its accumulation and its social ramifications, and, above all, control over resources. They express the ideas of public policies, the maintenance of the system, and the kind of political community to be promoted by a given political formation or political grouping.

One of the current intellectual tendencies of some scholars and policymakers is to equate democratic debates (for instance, the freedom of expression, human rights, and the struggle for economic and cultural independence) with multipartyism and dictatorship within the one-party state. This raises serious epistemological and policy questions as to our definitions and understanding of what democracy is or ought to be in an African context. A similar tendency is to equate any centralized social system with dictatorship, and any decentralized one, even one that does not have any participatory policies, with democracy. This creates confusion about what democracy is, or is not, and what it ought to be. What did one-party states, for instance, Chama Cha Mapinduzi (CCM) in Tanzania under Julius Nyerere, and the multiparty system under Mobutu of Congo-Zaïre or Paul Biya of Cameroon, have in common in democratic terms?

While social and economic conditions in most parts of Africa are worsening, the euphoria associated with the rise of popular and democratic movements continues to raise new expectations, hopes, and enthusiasm about the future of the new African societies as clearly expressed in the re-election of Mathieu Kérékou of Bénin in 1996, the 1995 elections in Ethiopia, the presidential elections of June 1993 in Nigeria, and in the CAR's people's participation in the presidential elections in 1993. However, the recent military mutinies in the CAR, recent military coup d'etats in Sierra Leone and in Congo-Brazzaville raised issue of the significance of such a participation. It should be noted, once again, that so far there are no significant economic and sociological data to support the assumption of positive correlations between democratic discourse and economic development in Africa.

For more than 20 years, the World Bank and the IMF worked with the highly centralized regimes, the civilian one-party states, and the military regimes. What the bank was interested in then was institutional stability; the nature and origins of such stability were of little importance. For instance, it was assumed that institutional stability would be able to maintain peace and order, pre-requisites for creating a working environment for the movement of goods and people. Yet maintaining this peace and order meant working closely with dictators, who, in most cases in Africa, appropriated national resources for their own security. This clearly shows the inconsistent deontology of the bank.

The bank was not interested in ethical issues because those issues are difficult to define and solve. It was assumed that institutional stability would guarantee the rational functioning of the market. It was more important to create or maintain the conditions in which a given country would be able to consistently service its outstanding debt and acquire more loans. Certainly, it is not accidental that loans were given systematically to states or presidents who did not even claim to practice or believe in democracy (for example, Nimeiry of the Sudan, Mobutu of Congo-Zaïre, Doe of Liberia, and Eyadema of Togo). Those dictators created a better-functioning environment for the bank than for the citizens.

In Africa, the bank worked with a very small number of government economists in departments of economy or finance, or in the offices of presidents or prime ministers, behind closed doors. Even within the same government or regime, the process of sharing information and getting input from others has been limited. Only a few technicians and politicians were involved in the decision making process regarding World Bank business in Africa, and the process of implementation was not based on the democratic ethos and principles. Even when selecting their targets, the SAPs did not systematically scrutinize national institutions. Governments did not provide much input to the formulation or implementation of the bank's policies. Even when the World Bank's designed policies were delivered in the national languages and with national political symbols, they still represented the ideas of the bank and the West. For the bank's programs to succeed, their policy must involve the beneficiaries. As Rebecca D. Petersen as said: "The policy process needs to be expanded to include all whom the policy affects directly or indirectly. The voices of youths, parents, and the community residents need to be heard and acted upon for policies to become more democratic. Authentic democratic participation is the key to ameliorating the conditions of society"(1995, 648). This is one of the most important challenges the World Bank and the IMF operations are facing in Africa. In the past, the bank advocated a liberal market and economy within a non-democratic environment. Now it has added good governance and human rights to its conditions for evaluating the dossiers of states that apply for loans.

CONCLUSION

Why is it that public policies, based on and defined within the framework of the SAPs, are producing terrible social and economic conditions in many parts of Africa? Despite the World Bank's rhetoric, there is no clear indication that programs of privatization, promoted by both the World Bank and the IMF, and implemented within the framework of multiparty democracy, are either succeeding in qualitatively transforming the productive forces of the people in Africa or substantially improving their living standards. What is clear is the significant increase in debt, which reached about $211 billion in 1995.

The operations of the SAPs have been essentially anti-democratic and anti-state planning. Thus, the assumptions of the bank and the IMF, and those of popular and democratic movements, have been permanently in conflict. The bank perceives Africa, from a market perspective, as a peripheral capitalist entity. In focusing on fiscal policies without looking at the global picture, its programs tend to weaken state initiatives for planning. In fact, fragile planning practices by the African state have been more of the instrument of political control than instruments of social management and constructive or progressive change. From the free market perspective, state planning is an impediment to order and stability. Rather than embracing state planning, the SAPs have sought to truncate it.

Although multiparty democracy has not been rooted in African political culture, recently the parliaments in some countries (for example, Bénin, Côte d'Ivoire, Congo-Brazzaville [before the explosive power struggle of 1997], and Kenya) have decided to become more involved in the SAPs' activities. Their intervention in order to make appropriate recommendations may not tear down the SAPs, but it is likely to alter some of the bank and the IMF rigidities and conditionalities. This intervention may also delay their implementation, if it is supported by genuine democratic struggles.

Theoretically, democratic discourse that is inclusive and holistic can systematically promote a diversity of views, the value of consensus, tolerance based on law and culture, and respect for individual and collective social rights and liberties. These factors that can potentially produce mechanisms through which social progress can occur. They can liberate minds, energize cultures, and promote individual and collective initiatives. Epistemological and historically, democratic discourse must be rooted in local conditions. Comparatively and functionally, its significance can be appreciated internationally. Without solid institutional planning based on participation from Africans, the SAPs will not be able to reach many people in a positive manner, and development will not occur in Africa. Clearly, Africa needs a restructuring that is promoted by state planning and supported by the ideals of democracy and local social demands. The tendencies of de-statization of Africa within the global economy, as represented by the SAPs of the World Bank and the IMF, cannot create mechanisms for appropriate planning. Contrary to the arguments of the bank, this de-statization, as a process of reinforcing Africa's past role, is not only an economic phenomenon; it is essentially an effort to further peripheralize Africa and diminish her potential to influence world political events for her advantages.

NOTES

1. "Africa is World Bank's 'Top Priority': James Wolfensohn Stresses Investment, Regional Integration during Second Trip to Continent," *Africa Recovery*, 10:4 (January–April 1997): 16.

2. Committee on Foreign Affairs, *Structural Adjustment in Africa: Insights from the Experiences of Ghana and Senegal* (Washington, D.C.: Government Printing Office, 1989), p. 3.

3. Most of the information in the first part of this chapter, especially the discussion on the SAPs, was drawn from the research project that the author co-conducted on "The Impact of Structural Adjustments on Higher Education in Africa." The project was sponsored by the Council for Development of Social Research (CODESRIA) in Africa and the final report was due in September 1996. The data were also taken from the author's co-published article: "Can African States Make Development Planning within the Current Structural Adjustment Programs and Struggle for Democracy?" *International Third World Studies Journal and Review* volume VIII (1996): 33–45.

4. World Bank, *Adjustment in Africa: Reforms, Results and the Road Ahead* (New York, Oxford University Press, 1994).

5. The World Bank, *Sub-Saharan African: From Crisis to Sustainable Growth*

(Washington, D.C.: The World Bank), 1989.

6.   World Bank, *Making Adjustment Work for the Poor* (Washington, D.C.: World Bank, 1990), p. 1.

7.   World Bank, *Adjustment in Africa*, p. 3.

8.   For further information on the unilinear and confirmist stages of economic development, see W. W. Rostow, *The Stages of Economic Growth, A Non-Communist Manifesto* (London: Cambridge University Press), 1960.

8

A General Conclusion: What Lessons from the Past and Where to Go from Here?

Presently, as articulated in this book, many types of democratic debates are being carried on in most parts of Africa. The nature of the debates, the actors involved in them, and the social conditions in which the actors live should be analyzed dialogically rather than linearly. The history of past democratic practices and of the emergence and re-emergence of dictatorships must be critically revisited to avoid reproducing the terrible mistakes of the past. These mistakes need to be avoided by an *esprit critique* ("a critical mind") of the history of ideas and political praxis for, as the philosopher George Santayana has noted, "Those who do not learn from their past mistakes are doomed to repeat them." What is the nature of the political project (political community and its ideologies) underlined or projected in the new democratic motion? How a given democratic process came about is an important issue that can help us determine whether or not some form of democracy is really on the horizon in Africa. However, for better or worse, it should be clearly recognized that some changes have taken place in many dimensions of African political life. This should not be intellectually or socially denied.

As discussed in several parts of this book, two intellectual positions have dominated the existing discourses on the democratization process and development (social progress) in Africa. Some have articulated their arguments via natural law reasoning, with the assumption that human beings are naturally endowed by "their Creator with certain inalienable Rights," including democracy. Other positions seem to come from an alternative theory close to a social contract theory. Within the natural law theory, as it seems to be closely related to physiocratic assumptions, one is entitled to democratic rights simply because one is a rational human being. One does not have to agree to honor these inalienable rights. Within the social contract reasoning, democracy is a social and historical phenomenon. It is a constructive agreement, a reflection of *logos* made by human beings to build society. It is also instrumental for higher purposes. Depending on the origin of a given society, in general, the social contract, as mutually agreed upon, is conceived of as a phenomenon that ought to enlighten the citizens and influence their cultural values.

But whose contract are we talking about? How is it reached? What is its content?

In practical terms, democracy as a part of natural laws and democracy as a social right can complement each other in policy matters. An inalienable right is a right only if it is intended to fulfill human happiness in a given social context according to the norms established by people in that social environment. It should be noted that, philosophically, happiness is also a transcendental concept. It is not a physically deterministic phenomenon. Democracy is a social phenomenon only if its social accomplishments are determined to be higher than its metaphysical assumptions. People must agree upon the terms of its realization and the values it carries out. Whether democracy is perceived, defined, or classified for analytical purposes as an instrumentalist phenomenon or as a normative one, what seems to be most important is that the people's right to *logos* (speech or reason) and to establish institutions of political debate is philosophically and politically linked with the rights to social life and its various process of reproduction. The ideal of democracy is ontologically good in itself and universal. It is *une idée force* ("a dynamic idea") has embodies philosophical elements of human equality and freedom. However, its appreciation and its applicability not only varies from one place to another, but it also depends on the conditions of a given milieu and its local forces. It is only at the policy level that the ideal of democracy becomes socially more valuable, as it is formulated to deal with or solve people's specific social problems at a given time. At that level, democracy as realism (or pragmatism) seems to be more of a product of a historical conditionality than this of the construction of idealists or universalists. In their discussions about democracy, concerned scholars have underlined the interactions between realist and idealist positions. Democracy, as defined here, has a certain level of permanent idealism, without which democracy cannot exist.

In Africa, the mandate for democracy, as expressed in the current languages of popular movements, is not a self-glorification, as was the case in the Republic of Plato in the 5th century B.C., where women, traders, and people of slave origins were only allowed to participate in the process of building the city-state (*polis*), but they were not entitled to the political rights (or privileges) of citizens. The *agora* ("marketplace") was a dynamic place for a naturally selected few. In Africa, the outcome of the democratic processes such as nominations, campaigns, elections, and debates and *le verbe politique* ("the political voice") should not be philosophically and socially separated from the principle of the right of all people to pursue the socially defined common good. Indeed, the democratization process is a social activity intended to promote the common and social good. This process should not merely be equated with the technical, ritual dimensions of voting or electing (procedural and delegative democracy).

This book articulates that intellectual discourses should not be simply about the question of whether democracy is on the horizon or is already here. Rather, it should also focus on what kind of democracy it ought to be. What are its origins? What are the rules of the democratic game? The specificities of the people's conditions and socio-political histories must be taken seriously as we analyze various democratic experiences in the world and plan to make some important decisions about where to go from here.

Why is it that African presidents, elected or non-elected, do not wish to retire peacefully from their presidential palaces, even those who appear to be relatively enlightened, such as Bernard Mugabe of Zimbabwe; Abdou Diouf of Senegal; General Etienne Eyadema of Togo; and Soglo, the former President of Bénin? The late president Mobutu Sese Seko of Zaïre (the Democratic Republic of Congo) had to be forced out, struggling until the last minute to retain the title of president. Mobutu finished his career as bandit and nationless.

The response to the question above is complex, and it requires a careful understanding of how the African state relates to society, and how both state and society interact with the Western powers in the global economy. In the case of Mobutu, for example, one could say that he built his confidence in retaining power on the nature of the military and financial support that he enjoyed for more than 30 years from his patrons in the North.

Popular movements have continued to expose the mortality of the states and their leaders. Even the late *vieux* or traditional chiefs like Félix Houphouët-Boigny of Côte d'Ivoire did not completely die like gods. African heads of state are forced to carefully watch the directions of popular movements. Even Bashir of the Sudan, who is surrounded by elements of Islamic fundamentalism, Paul Biya of Cameroon, or Daniel arap Moi of Kenya, all of whom have resisted the idea of the *force de l'histoire* ("the historical force") are not able to stop this process entirely. People have openly engaged in political debate about the nature of their society and the civil society to be rebuilt, including the future of their old and new heads of state and their political parties and organizations. Moreover, political parties, as expressions of liberal democracy or bourgeois democracy, have mushroomed in many parts of Africa. Ten years ago, it was hard to think that the African National Congress (ANC) or the South West People's Organization (SWAPO) would become their countries' ruling parties with new liberal constitutions. One can affirm that the political atmosphere has become, at least symbolically, more relaxed and healthier than ever before, even for the ruling classes themselves. What does that mean in terms of the significance of multiparty democracy in people's lives? Will the current movements and parties create real political and social democracy in Africa? What will they do to eradicate poverty? How long will this political activism last? What are the possible directions?

Despite the fact that "the gross domestic product in eighteen African countries which have adapted the SAPs grew by five percent or more in 1996, while Africa's overall GDP growth rose from under three percent in 1995 to over four percent,"[1] this growth does not seem to have had a visible positive impact on the majority of African people's lives in terms of improvement of their social conditions.

In contemporary politics, especially in the West, the concepts of political pluralism and liberal democracy are interrelated phenomena. Despite the controversial nature of the concept of political pluralism among various schools of thought, there is an agreement concerning its usage. It denotes, within a given political environment, some ideals which can be generalized—for instance, a certain level of political openness, the existence of various forms of political organizations, and the struggle for respect for the community or collective group and individual interests and rights. It is a struggle for power orchestrated by various political groupings, which is channeled through legal means and institutions. However, it should be emphasized that the form such struggles takes varies according to the dynamics of the local objective conditions of each milieu, including its history and the composition of its social forces. Political pluralism is not merely a behavior of political tolerance by the state and the ruling class; rather, it is a result of the effort of political forces to institutionalize their opposition to the ruling classes and dictators and establish the criteria of how a political community ought to be collectively organized and built; it is the process through which the circulation of state power becomes more or less impersonal and more open, and a certain level of political competition is introduced and maintained in the rules of political games. It creates the consciousness that acquiring power is not a natural process. This political consciousness is expected to encourage dialogue among various social forces in a given society. It can also help people identify their own priorities, and it can force the state to democratize development projects and political institutions.

Political pluralism and the struggle for democracy, as articulated by the media, have become part of the political discourses in most countries in Africa, even where the debates, as in Uganda, have not greatly expanded (on the Western standard). While these debates have become relatively open, intense, and legalized, in some cases, they have led to political violence. The popular movements and political parties that started early, but exploded in the 1990s, demanded the resignation of dictator political leaders like Mobutu of Zaïre and Eyadema of Togo. Mobutu Sese Seko and Moussa Traoré in Mali are examples of former African leaders who did not pay attention to their people's problems. However, even Dénis Sassou Nguesso of the Congo, who has some background in labor organization and activism, did not predict the intensity of people's anger against his dictatorship practices and about underdevelopment. Thus, these dictators were trapped by the people's anger and hunger. These kinds of movements are not completely new in African politics. What is new then? The dominant philosophy behind political pluralism and the global social and economic context make the current movements towards democracy different from those of the past.

In the 1950s and 1960s, a mixture of popular and nationalist movements succeeded in creating social and political spaces that became more or less conducive to some kinds of political pluralism or multiparty democracy à l'Européenne. Most of these movements raised issues of economic and political rights: for instance, the right of access to land; the right to preserve African value systems; cultural rights; the right to vote; and for the African elites, the right to share powers with the Western elite and the right to self-determination. Finally, either through negotiations or armed struggles, the African people partially gained their political rights. The struggles to acquire these rights became testimonies for the recognition of the majority of Africans as citizens of their own countries and their right to travel in their own country without having to carry an authorization card or a laissez-passer.

Those rights were quickly violated, as people with uniforms and guns took over state power, with or without external support. In addition, it should be remembered that military dictatorships were not historical accidents. They were established partially because Africans accepted becoming nominally political independent without restructuring their economies and societies. Africans did not control their own destiny. Dictators were either imposed on Africans or supported by some imperialist states so that Africa could continue to serve industrial countries more effectively, especially their elites and their workers.

States that are economically, technologically, and militarily powerful teleologically created the underdevelopment destiny. How did this happen? Things are more complicated and complex than they usually appear to be because underdevelopment is not simply a product of one person. A generalized answer is not elaborated upon in this book. However, some elements of a general explanation can be made concerning the nationalist agenda, whether it is Mobutu's type or Eyadema's.

The claims of most popular movements, for instance, self-determination or self-reliance, which theoretically seem to have been more democratic than those of the petty bourgeois movements, were used by the emerging elites simply for advancing particular class interests that first of all centered on caricatured power. The struggle for political independence and decolonization was disassociated from economic decolonization. All leaders and members of the elite class (the *évolués*) in the Congo-Leopoldville, the late *Mze* (old used in a respectful manner) Jomo Kenyatta group in Kenya, the *"élites"* of the *Rassemblement Démocratique Africain* (RDA) in francophone West Africa, or the pan-Africanist Kwame Nkrumah in Ghana were convinced that political independence would eventually lead to economic or cultural independence. Could policies and social and political conditions inherited from colonial structures be automatically conducive to further independence in other domains of African life? This depends a great deal on how a given country earned its independence, the nature of its post-colonial leadership, the dynamism of its rural classes, its political economy, and its policies.

Soon after independence, many nationalists, especially leftist radicals, realized that the law of physics that dictates that "things do not change by themselves," and the law of the modern state that maintains the "immortality of the interests of state," laws which are considered by people in power to be ontologically rational, clashed with each other. Some nationalists attempted to make changes in the political and social conditions of their milieux, and Western industrial states, in the name of global capitalism, resisted any new moves in this direction. This clash was very much reflected in the direct interventionism by the industrial powers and multinational corporations in Africa to control, promote, and protect their own interests. These interventions were essentially done culturally, militarily, and politically. The contradictions of global capitalism, as the interventions intensified after the 1970s in the African political economy, indicated how far this clash can go. The main losers have been the millions of African peasants, women, youth, and lumpen-proletarians who have no jobs and cannot compete in the international labor market.

Furthermore, within the international division of labor, many states and ruling classes opted to continue with the African classic role of producers of raw materials and consumers of imported goods from industrial countries. Here, the good will or good behavior of any political actor does not necessarily lead to structural change. The law of nature, or the so-called invisible hand (the market), regulates social relations, and Africa's role has become truncated in many parts of the continent. As long as one is a consumer, one must accept the consequences that come with this role.

Although African markets can also compete with other markets, the politics of industrial nations concerning markets have not allowed real competition to happen. International markets do not function in a political vacuum, as some economists want us to believe, and world markets are highly politicized. They are highly protected by the national politics in the industrial countries. For instance, tariffs, export-import relations, and private bank loans all play the unwritten diplomatic role of their prime investors, whether these investors are states or individual citizens. African states have not been able to penetrate these politicized markets in a positive way. With high-tech industrialization, marketization, and regionalization of the global economy, they may not even succeed in penetrating these markets any time soon. African commodities are marginalized, not necessarily because of their alleged low quality, but because of the low visibility of Africa in international political debates, and because of the politics associated with underdevelopment. Africans must know and decide collectively what they want to produce and where they want to sell. The decision to do this is, above all, political.

Neo-colonial politics in the 1960s and 1970s contributed to the rise of militarization, which made the existing fragments of multiparty politics and bourgeois democracy disappear and created the conditions in which Africa's economic dependence deepened. The conspiracy theory, which has been controversial and rejected by some scholars, has some significance here. For instance, in the Congo-Leopodville (the Democratic Republic of Congo), economic decolonization was consciously separated from the political agenda of the Belgian administrators. With the exception of a few nationalists, most of the évolués who took over power were trying to copy the policies of the European powers. Thus, they did not have any relevant or clear social economic agenda for the Congo. The *Union Minière du Haut Katanga (UMK)*, for example, was still run like an independent state when the Congo acquired its nominal political independence. The *Loi Fondamentale* ("fundamental law") was clearly a conspiratorial document. In countries where colonial powers did not succeed in structurally maintaining the economic status quo, in fighting nationalists, the colonialists literally destroyed the economic base and infrastructures based on the notion that "If we can't have it, nobody will." Algeria, Kenya, and Mozambique are some of the best known examples where this savagery occurred.

At the national level, some states opted for nationalization, or Africanization. This policy was used as an instrument of the state and the ruling classes to politically manage some dimensions of the national economy. The state gained some access to foreign capital, which was used to maintain the status quo and crush the opposition and democratic movements. Mobutu was the champion of this policy.

In many cases, political pluralism and democratic movements have been antithetical to political nationalization. Nationalization became another political avenue through which neo-colonial rulers used raw power to spread their dictatorship principles and consolidate their powers. For those who chose a cooperative approach with the industrial powers, the borrowed capital and foreign investments contributed to intensifying their dictatorial practices, whether civilian or military. These investments, if any, were not seriously intended to contribute to the development of human equality, which is the basis for democracy.

Foreign capital in Africa has not created the conditions for democracy. On the contrary, foreign capital's monopoly in the African political economy cannot naturally operate on the principle of democracy. Cheap labor and exploitation are imbedded in the monopoly and the dictatorship of foreign capital. Democracy, as a process of people's participation in the management and the decision making of their institutions and their affairs, cannot be engendered from the spirit and operation of the monopoly of foreign capital. In short, both nationalization and a cooperative approach with the industrial powers (as occurred in most former French colonies) created political absolutism and personalized regimes. As a consequence, the African masses temporarily lost their battles against the enemies of democracy who, until recently, used military means and unpopular policies to crush popular movements. But this was only temporary, *une partie remise* ("still unsolved problem") because the masses have to struggle first for survival in their harsh social, political, and economic conditions.

Economic dependence is the most important factor in the creation and maintenance of political absolutism, and this has retarded African progress for more than 40 years. It does not allow local democratic forces to continue their struggle for both economic and political rights. The austerity programs preached and imposed by the International Monetary Fund (IMF) and the World Bank cannot genuinely advance democratic conditions. They only prepare the ground for more social miseries, uprisings, and political instability. For the IMF to obtain efficiency in the systems of production and management, there is a need for cutting budgets and services, actions which produce unemployment and create 1,000 percent inflation in some cases, as well as high interest rates in debt-service and balancing budgets. As viewed by the IMF, the misery of human beings has been less important than the technical concept of development.

Popular movements have been fighting the absolutist and highly centralized state powers in Africa since the 1960s, despite the degradation of social conditions. Even in a desperate case like Zaïre, elements of the working class, especially market women in urban areas, and students protested against Mobutu's policies and his brutal security system. What happened in Côte d'Ivoire between February and April of 1990 is also relevant. Among the social forces that protested against the deteriorating economic conditions were young soldiers who could have taken power if they decided to do so. There was a short period of near state power vacuum (though not constitutionally) in Côte d'Ivoire when all processes of struggle reached their highest level. However, these forces, including the young soldiers, were not interested in challenging the *Parti Démocratique de la Côte d'Ivoire* (PDCI) and its monopoly of power; rather, they were interested in the improvement of their social conditions and also in maintaining loyalty to the culture of stability, as it had been established by the ruling elite. They were against the policy implications of the IMF and against the domestic policies of cutting expenditures and subsidies without significantly improving the living conditions of the majority of the people. Some changes in Africa, including the independence of Namibia and the election of Nelson Mandela as president in South Africa have produced some *facteurs catalyseurs* that have brought some hopes and illusions that things could change for the better. These hopes, however, have not been entertained by many states. Indeed, hopes have turned into desperation in some countries, as states have started to fight back against the popular movements' demands. The combination of a lack of democracy and excessive poverty led to the total collapse of Liberia and Somalia, the recent military mutinies in the CAR, and the military coup d'etat in Sierra Leone in May 1997. Despite the failure of popular movements to save countries from collapsing in many parts of Africa, they have gained legal ground to struggle for political pluralism and democracy. They have forced states to revise their constitutions or to set up new rules for multiparty politics. The political reforms that have taken place thus have two origins: (1) the dynamism of the local forces and conditions (including the contradictions within the global system or *l'empire du mal*—"the evil empire"—as Samir Amin called it at the local level); and (2) changes in international political conditions.

One of the main differences between current political reforms and those that took place during the colonial period in the 1950s and 1960s is that many recent movements did not necessarily start with the existing state or state apparatus. On the contrary, many of them are essentially anti-state in terms of their behavior and their relationship with society. For instance, the Alliance of Democratic Forces for the Liberation of Congo, led by President Laurent-Désiré Kabila of the Democratic Republic of Congo (ADFL), operated outside of the rules of civil society and the state structures.

The actors and the political environment have changed in the new movements. Although some petty bourgeois national movements of four decades ago were linked with popular movements in the rural areas, generally most of them were associated with a state or an urban setting. The current movements have risen out of the worsening social and political conditions in Africa.

Generally, Africans are among the most patient people on the face of the earth. The culture of tolerance that characterizes Africa has been challenging the individualism and values of the commodity relations of the West. People are finally rejecting tyranny, as was the case recently in the Democratic Republic of Congo. This is a sign that the social and political conditions that the tyrants have created have become unacceptable to most human beings.

In addition to the local factors, the international atmosphere has rapidly been changing. With the end of the Cold War and the militaristic attempts of the United States to impose its own order on a world that is socially polycentric, the history of the world is being written backward. Instead of encouraging the development of real political pluralism and democracy, Washington, especially the Republicans and their cronies have subtly opted against pluralism and democracy. Are genuine political pluralism and democracy possible in the current economic dependence of Africa?

Since the 1960s, countries that have socially, politically, and economically been more dependent on foreign powers have also been less democratic in their behavior and policies. Those that have accumulated more debts also tend to respond more violently against popular struggles for political pluralism and democracy. Economic dependence is itself a non-democratic force. It cannot create any conditions that are conducive to a genuine democracy, the advancement of human equality, equal distribution of resources and of powers, and full political participation. This dependence embodies contradictions that cannot enhance the emancipation of leaders and their policies. In the conditions of dependence, African leaders tend to hide their actions and policies behind a liberal economic argument. Can free political discourse succeed in improving the social and political conditions of the majority of people?

One should not confuse democracy and political pluralism. Democracy is a process of actualizing freedom and human equality. This process can occur with or without political pluralism "à l'Européenne" or "à l'Americaine." Before colonization, most African societies were democratic, but they did not develop party politics that exist in today's democracies.

However, contemporary African societies are historically different from pre-colonial African societies by the nature of their political formations, their economies, and their incorporation into the global capitalist economy. The African political community of the 1990s is composed of various states that are artificial, fragile, and struggling to be immortal; thus, they are maintained militarily at the expense of the majority of the people. Their objectives are centered more on power than on collective social progress and community programs. They are qualitatively different from traditional societies, which were generally centered on community interests and some harmonious principles of social and political organizations.

The existence of internal contradictions within the African traditional systems cannot be denied. The modern state in Africa requires some formula of political pluralism through which people can seek for a better system of power sharing and distribution of resources. The mission of this political pluralism is to be the *gendarme* ("police officer") of democracy. The neo-colonial political history of Africa shows that not all forms of political pluralism produce or protect democracy. World capitalism is not likely to allow the development of any genuine political pluralism in Africa.

Pluralistic political discourses in Africa should be accompanied by debates on the structure of African economies and military systems, and they should not be separated from economic and social issues. With Zäire's $14 billion of debt, for example, its high rate of debt-service for more than 80 percent of its revenue, its lack of infrastructure, its total political corruption at all levels of society, and most of all, its dependence on foreign capital and the military, could Mobutu, for instance, contribute to the establishment of a genuine democracy? Despite the good will of president Henri Konan Bédié, and his determined efforts at diversifying economic relationships between Côte d'Ivoire and other countries, can liberal democracy function effectively here with the ruling party, *Parti Démocratique de la Côte d'Ivoire* monopolizing most of the state resources, and with the state's deep dependence on France for administrative decision making, military and technical assistance, and capital? Is Jerry Rawlings of Ghana capable of becoming democratic? Senegal, for instance, has been technically pluralistic and democratic longer than many countries in Africa, and the political discourse here has been one of the most open, stable, and interesting ones. With the existence of an active parliament and visible opposition parties, does the Senegalese state policy making process and its implementation reflect political pluralism and real democracy? For instance, did the Senegalese government fully and honestly explain the true reasons for its military involvement in the Gulf War, where they joined other countries to fight Iraq's Hussein under the order of the U.S. President George Bush and where more than 80 Senegalese soldiers died in a plane crash?

Democracy plus economic dependence is only a short-lived phenomenon, an illusion of life, a pairing that creates a bad marriage. In terms of improving African social conditions and developing talents, this situation of economic and cultural dependency will not lead to promote an engaging democracy.

Democracy is not only a political process in which people formally participate in the institutions of their country or are given some political rights, it also is a mechanism through which people struggle for their total and genuine independence. It is a right for self-actualization, determination, improvement, and empowerment. It cannot be fully realized in conditions of excessive dependence. Even in the context of globalization, real political pluralism in Africa has to come with a certain degree of economic de-linking (not autarky) from the global capitalist structures. This is the way Africans may re-orient their economy, identify their new priorities, and set up their new agenda for social progress. Africans should not miss this obvious opportunity, and they should also politicize their own markets if they wish to progress in their own economies and technologies. This politization may really make sense if the activities and policies of the African regional economic organizations are framed with a political vision of unity.

Economic dependence is an important factor in the failure of the policies promoted by political pluralistic and democratic movements. Political parties in Africa that depend financially and ideologically on the metropolitan countries also cannot escape from the general law of dependence. They may disregard, in operating, the objective conditions of their milieux and may consciously or unconsciously represent the interests of foreign domination through the parties of the metropolitan powers. The danger of this is that they may read history and the contradictions of the local conditions through the glasses of foreign political parties, and this would weaken their vision and policies for the advancement of democracy, which is badly needed in Africa.

Self-reliance is the *sine qua non* for the success of political pluralism and democracy in Africa. Unfortunately, many African states have turned away from self-reliance as a guide for a genuine political democracy. Rather, they have embraced Structural Adjustment Programs as the magic formula of their effort to take off. With the negative social impacts of these programs on people's purchasing power and the lack of self-reliant projects, unfortunately it may not take long for the military to brutally attempt to reassert itself on the political scene in Africa.

Real democracy cannot occur when only the elites control states and when the ownership of the means of production is still in the hands of multinationals and foreign powers. Furthermore, there will be no democracy if people are prevented from participating in the political affairs of their country or community—for instance, in controlling and managing their major economic resources.

Democracy is not merely a slogan, as it has often been used in Africa. Rather, it is a social activity and a commitment to higher objectives: the building of a participatory society with respect to laws, to African value systems, and to human dignity. It has to fight misery, starvation, sexism, and social injustices. The democratization process must deal with ways to introduce debates about these issues into social institutions as soon as possible. The debates about the relationships between state policies, people's claims and expectations, and the functions and structures of the international political economy must be at the core of the discourses concerning the democratization process in Africa.

The most important political problem in Africa is poverty. Political discourses will not give a global picture of African conditions and realities without critically examining African economies. Democracy and development, as well as social progress in Africa, will not come as a result of the isolated efforts of the national petty bourgeoisie. Rather, they may be produced as a result of the political struggles between the popular movement and social class coalition, and as a result of the formulation and implementation of social planning.

NOTE

1. "Africa is World Bank's 'Top Priority,' James Wolfensohn Stresses Investment, Regional Integration during Second Trip to Continent," *Africa Recovery* 10: 4 (January–April 1997): 16.

Selected Bibliography

"Africa is World Bank's 'Top Priority,': James Wolfensohn Stresses Investment, Regional Integration during Second Trip to Continent." *Africa Recovery* 10, no. 4 (January–April 1997): 16.

Ake, Claude. *Social Science As Imperialism*. Ibadan, Nigeria: Ibadan University Press, 1982.

____. "Democracy and Development." *West Africa* (April 1990)

____.*The New World Order: The View from the South*. Lagos, Nigeria: Malthouse Press, 1992.

____. *Democracy and Development in Africa*. Washington, D.C., 1996.

Amin, Samir. *Développement du capitalisme en Côte d'Ivoire*. Paris: Editions de Minuit, 1967.

Anderson, Samantha, trans. *Thomas Sankara Speaks: The Burkina-Faso Revolution*. New York: Pathfinder, 1988.

Anyang' Nyong'o, Peter. "Discourses on Democracy in Africa." Paper read at the Seventh General Assembly of CODESRIA, Dakar, Senegal 10–14 February 1992.

Apter, E. David. "The Role of Traditionalism in the Political Modernization of Ghana and Uganda," *World Politics*, 13, no. 1 (1965): 45–48.

Apter, E. David. *The Politics of Modernization*. Chicago, University of Chicago Press, 1965.

Apter, E. David and Carl G. Rosberg. *Political Development and the New Realism in Sub-Saharan Africa*. Charlottesville and London: University Press of Virginia, 1994.

Axelos, Kostas. *Alienation, Praxis, and Technen in the Thought of Karl Marx*. Austin, TX: University of Texas Press, 1976.

Badara, Diouf. "Coup d'État: Panorama d'un phénomène inquiétant." *Le Soleil*, (Vendredi 14 juin 1996): 7–9.

Badarat, Leon P. *Political Ideologies: Their Origins and Impact*. Englewood Cliffs, NJ: Prentice Hall, 1994.

Barkan, Joel D., ed. *Beyond Capitalism Versus Socialism in Kenya and Tanzania*. Boulder, Co: Lynne Rienner Publishers, 1994.

Bentsi-Enchill, Nii K. "Modest Economic Upturn." *Africa Recovery* 8, no. 3 (December 1994): 1, 13.

Betts, K. Richard. *Conflict After the Cold War: Arguments on Causes of War and Peace*. New York: Macmillan, 1994.

Bienen, Henry. "Leaders, Violence, and the Absence of Change in Africa." *Political Science Quarterly* 108, no. 2 (Summer 1993): 271–282.

Bobb, F. Scott. *A Historical Dictionary of Zaïre*. Metuchen, NJ: Scarecrow Press, 1988.

Boyer, William W. "Reflections on Democratization." *PS: Political Science and Politics* (September 1992).

Bratton, Michael. "Are Competitive Elections Enough?" *Africa Demos* 3, no. 4 (March 1995).

Brecher, Jeremy, and Tim Costello. *Global Village or Global Pillage: Economic Reconstruction from the Bottom Up*. Boston, MA: South End Press, 1994.

Callaghy, M. Thomas. "Africa: Falling Off the Map." *Current History* 93, no. 579 (January 1994): 31–36.

Chege, Michael. "The Kenya December 1992 General Elections: Opposition Leaders Play into the Hands of the Ruling Kanu Party." *CODESRIA Bulletin* 1 (1993).

Decalo, Samuel. *Coups and Army Rule in Africa: Studies in Military Style*. New Haven, CT: Yale University Press, 1976.

Dyckman, John. "Three Crises of American Planning." In *Planning Theory in the 1980s*, edited by George Sternlieb and Robert Burchell. New Brunswick, NJ: Rutgers Center for Urban Policy Research, 1975.

Eisenstadt, S.N. *Modernization: Protest and Change*. Englewood Cliffs, NJ: Prentice Hall, 1966.

Fanon, Frantz. *The Wretched of the Earth*. New York: Grove Weidenfeld, 1991.

Furley, Oliver. *Conflict in Africa*. London: I. B. Tauris Publishers, 1995.

Giomee, Hermann. "Democracy in South Africa." *Political Science Quarterly* 110, no. 1 (Spring 1995): 83–104.

Grey, Robert D., ed. *Democratic Theory and Post-Communist Change*. Upper Saddle River, NJ: Prentice Hall, 1997.

Gutteridge, W. F. *Military Regimes in Africa*. London: Methuen, 1975.

Hague, Rod, Martin Harrop, and Shaun Reslin. *Political Science: Comparative Introduction*. New York: St. Martin's Press, 1992.

Huntington, Samuel. *Political Order in Changing Societies*. New Haven, CT: Yale University Press, 1968.

Ihonvbere, Julius O. "Military and Political Engineering under Structural Adjustment: The Nigerian Experience Since 1985." *Journal of Political and Military Sociology* 20, no. 1 (Summer 1991): 107–131.

Ki-Zerbo, Joseph. *Histoire de l'Afrique noire: d'hier à demain*. Paris: A Hatier, 1972.

Lione, Sali. "African Debate on Reforms Shifting Focus." *Africa Recovery* (June 1995).

Lumumba-Kasongo, Tukumbi. "Katangan Secessionist Movement, Manifestation of the Western Interests or Internal Power Struggle?" *Journal of African Studies* 15, nos. 3 and 4 (Fall/Winter 1988–89): 101–109.

_____. *Nationalistic Ideologies, Their Policy Implications and The Struggle for Democracy in African Politics*. Lewiston, NY: Edwin Mellen Press, 1991a.

_____. "State, Economic Crisis, and Educational Reform in Côte d'Ivoire." In *Understanding Educational Reform in Global Context: Economy, State, and Ideology*, edited by Mark B. Ginsburg, 257–284. New York: Garland Publishing, 1991b.

_____. *Political Re-mapping of Africa: Transnational Ideology and Re-definition of Africa in World Politics*. Lanham, MD: University Press of America, 1994.

_____ and Kent A. Klitgaard. "Can African States Make Development Planning within the Current Structural Adjustment Programs and Struggle for Democracy?" *International Third World Studies Journal and Review* 8 (1996): 33–45.

Martin, Guy. "Revolutionary Democracy, Socio-Political Conflict and Militarization in Burkina Faso, 1983–88." In *Democracy and the One-Party State in Africa*, edited by

Dani Wadada Nabudere and Peter Meyns, 57-77. Harbourg: Germany, Institut für Afrika-Kunde: 1989.

Mengisteab, Kidan and Bikubolajeh Logan. *Beyond Economic Liberalization in Africa: Structural Adjustment and the Alternative.* London: Zed Books, 1995.

Nnoli, Okwudiba. *Ethnicity and Democracy in Africa: Intervening Variables.* Centre for Advanced Social Science (CASS) Occasional Monograph Series no. 4. Oxford: Malthouse Press, 1994.

Novicki, A. Margaret. "UN Security Council Focuses Spotlight on African Conflicts." *Africa Report* 11, no. 2 (October 1997): 1–5.

Nzongola-Ntalaja, Georges. *Revolution and Counter-Revolution in Africa: Essays in Contemporary Politics.* London: Zed Books, 1987.

Nzouankeu, Jacques Mariel. "The Role of the National Conference in the Transition to Democracy in Africa: The Cases of Bénin and Mali." *Issue: A Journal of Opinion* 21, nos. 1–2 (1993): 44–50.

Obeng, Ernest E. *Ancient Ashanti Chieftaincy.* Tema, Ghana: Ghana Publishing Corporation, 1986.

Olaniyan, R. Omotayo. *Foreign Aid, Self-Reliance, and Economic Development in West Africa.* Westport, CT: Praeger, 1996.

Osaghae, Eghosa. *Ethnicity and Its Management in Africa: The Democratization Link.* Centre for Advanced Social Science (CASS) Occasional Monograph no. 2. Oxford: Malthouse Press, 1994.

Parenti, Michael. "Fascism: The False Revolution." Lecture given on the Alternative Radio, Berkeley, California, September 23, 1995.

Petersen, Rebecca D. "Expert Policy in Juvenile Justice: Patterns of Claimsmaking and Issues of Power in a Program of Construction." *Policy Studies Journal* 23, no. 4 (1995): 636–651.

Rostow, W. W. *The Stages of Economic Growth: A Non-Communist Manifesto.* London: Cambridge University Press, 1960.

Salim, Ahmed Salim. "Link National, International Democratization: OAU's Salim." *Africa Recovery* 4, no. 2 (July–September 1990): 29.

Sandbrook, Richard. *The Politics of Africa's Economic Recovery.* Cambridge: Cambridge University Press, 1993.

Shivji, Issa. "The POs and the NGOs: Reflections on the Place of the Working People in the Battle for Democracy." *CODESRIA Bulletin* 4 (1990).

So, Y. Alvin. *Social Change and Development: Modernization, Dependency, and World System Theories.* Newbury Park, CA: Sage Publications, 1990.

Tshiyembe, Mwayila. "Etude Comparée de nouvelles institutions constitutionnelles africaines: Ignorance du modèle négro-africain de société postnationale, néoconstitutionnalisme de pacotille et absence de l'esprit des lois." *Présence Africaine* 156 (2ème Semestre, 1997): 37–98.

Wallerstein, Immanuel. *The World Politics of the World Economy: The States, the Movements and the Civilizations.* New York: Cambridge University Press, 1984.

Wamba-dia-Wamba, Ernest. "The Experience of Struggle in the People's Republic of Congo." In *Popular Struggles for Democracy in Africa,* edited by Peter Anyang' Nyong'o, 96–110. London and New Jersey: Zed Books, 1987.

West Africa. Selected Issues between 1985 and 1997, West Africa Publishing Co.

World Bank. *Making Adjustment Work for the Poor.* Washington, D.C.: World Bank, 1990.

World Bank. *Adjustment in Africa: Reforms, Results and the Road Ahead.* New York: Oxford University Press, 1994.

World Bank. International Bank for Reconstruction and Development/World Bank. *World Development Report 1995*. Oxford: Oxford University Press, 1995.
World Resources Institute. *World Resources 1994–95*. Oxford: Oxford University Press, 1994.

Index

About the Author

TUKUMBI LUMUMBA-KASONGO is Herbert J. Charles and Florence Charles Faegre Professor of Political Science and Chair of the Department of International Studies at Wells College, Senior Fellow at the Institute for African Development at Cornell University, Visiting Scholar in the Department of City and Regional Planning at Cornell University, and Director of CEPARRED. He has taught throughout Africa and the United States and has published extensively on international relations, social movements, and structural adjustment programs in Africa. He is the author of *The Dynamics of Economic and Political Relations Between Africa and Foreign Powers*: *A Study in International Relations*.

ISBN 0-275-96087-0

HARDCOVER BAR CODE